The Shift

WALTER A. BEEDE

Beede Baseball Publishing LLC
Lynn MA 01902

https://www.baseballprocess.com

CONTENTS

FOREWORD

by A Baseball Mom

I became acquainted with Walter on Twitter where I found many of his tweets, coach interviews, and commentaries to be insightful, well informed, and kinder than most whose business it is to develop youth baseball players and assist high school players in finding a college program. Walter was looking at the whole landscape of baseball in the USA, from youth to the MLB, and was not afraid to respectfully criticize some of the directions in which baseball was heading. I dug around online and saw that he has college coaching experience, has two sons who played at the college level, and one who is in the MLB. Those are pretty good credentials! Walter reached out to me and asked about my experiences with college baseball, and a very good discussion ensued. He told me about the book he was writing and sent me a few draft chapters. I quickly devoured the chapters and appreciated his insights into the big business of youth travel baseball. When I got to the chapters on college baseball, I felt someone else saw what I was seeing. It was a relief to have an expert put into words what I as a novice parent was piecing together.

Part of the reason I turned to Twitter was to gain insights into all the paradigm shifts in college baseball. I wanted to understand and heal from the crushing disappointment I felt with regards to how and why my son was cut from his college baseball program. Walter asked if I would be willing to do a YouTube interview. I declined because I knew my son would not be comfortable exposing what is essentially his story in the tight-knit world of college baseball. Then Walter asked if I would write something for his book. That felt better to me. I can write respectfully and anonymously. I only have one son who is already a lifelong devote of baseball. If I can help one parent understand the turbulent landscape of college baseball, then I have done my job in sharing what I have learned.

Please note that I have the upmost regard for college coaches and their sincere efforts to develop student-athletes and winning teams. Between the NIL (name, image, and likeness policy), prominent college programs conference hopping after TV money, the poaching of players, the transfer portal bonanza, recruiting changes, COVID's impact, and the musical chairs of coaching jobs; it's a demanding profession in a changing, rough-and-tumble landscape. And we haven't even gotten to the coaching part! Hats off to anyone passionate enough to take on the monumental job of college coaching!

And hats off to all the young players who have baseball dreams for themselves in this overly public fishbowl of youth and collegiate baseball. My son is crazy about baseball. His pals also love the game and derive a special joy from playing no matter the level. A boy and his baseball are a beautiful thing! I see how much joy baseball fans get from engaging with their favorite players and teams. I see the joy they find introducing their own children to the game, and to baseball's history that goes right along with the history of the United States. In critiquing the current state of baseball from youth to the MLB, Walter Beede is attempting to help preserve the wholesomeness of the youth game. He's helping parents change youth baseball's direction with their power of the purse and to make sound decisions about their child's baseball development. Prospective college recruits and their parents need to know Beede's analysis of the recruiting transformations in collegiate baseball that have significant drawbacks for high schooled aged youth. Beede details the stranglehold that money, winning, and big business have on America's favorite pastime. In that same spirit, I hope to encourage parents to watch carefully and move forward with great caution in buying all that is being marketed to you and your son(s) at any level. Here's our family's story.

My son absolutely loved his freshman year of the college program he committed to early in high school. He loved everything about it: the school, the coaches, the staff, and the players. He worked his butt off. He was full of joy and practiced all the time. He volunteered whenever a request for help came from a coach or player. The head coach told him at the end of Fall semester that he embodied the program. The coach told him he was a joy to have on the team. My son was all in! He never would have left the program—whether he started or not. Our son was in college for the student-athlete experience. My husband and I also wanted the college route for our son. We are not baseball people and researched the hell out of the field as novices, carefully researching college programs. We asked a lot of questions. We saw shark-infested waters ahead if our son was able to get to the next level (MiLB), but felt college was the best of both worlds. It would develop our son into a responsible young man with multiple life opportunities and give him a great shot at reaching his dream of playing professional baseball. Little did we know that the shark-infested waters of shrinking opportunity, big business, money, and winning-at-all-costs had engulfed college baseball—that everything was about to change.

It came as a shock when our son was cut from the team at the end of June, after his freshman year of college. Close to half the team was cut. Only a few players left of their own accord for greener pastures, likely poached by other similar programs with more lucrative offers (i.e., playing time, NIL money, and lastly scholarship.) Before our son attended college, my husband and I followed the team for several years. We noted a handful of kids left every year, which is normal for such an elite program. However, cutting half of the team was a different trend. Why? What has happened in college baseball when ethical coaches and programs behave in ways that are justifiable in promotional messaging, but are seemingly unethical towards the young men they profess to mentor and develop into responsible, college-educated adult US citizens?

Tectonic shifts in baseball at all levels have contributed to the paradigm shifts away from the traditional student-athletes as we understood them to be. Even though that was not a risk-free endeavor, we were comfortable with our son's drive and ability. We also confirmed our assessments from experienced, trusted sources. Add in the additional year of eligibility due to COVID for all 2020 college baseball players—these lucky young men given an extra year of eligibility, and coaches salivating at the prospects of older, more experienced players—and that left most incoming high school baseball players downright unlucky. Mine was one of those unlucky kids.

Our son entered the Transfer Portal towards the end of June with about a month to find another college and baseball program. Consider that most adults who are laid off from professional fields take three to six months or more to find another job. These young men who are semi-professionals (they are certainly not amateurs nor hobbyists!) had a few weeks to find another job. The competition was fierce. At that time there were over 2,000 players in the Transfer Portal. That number would balloon to over 3,000. What came next was perhaps the worst part of our son being cut.

Our son has a sunny, forward-looking CAN-DO disposition. Grateful for the experience he had in his freshman year, our son got to work immediately, searching for another college baseball program where he could earn playing time. The head coach who just cut him from the team graciously agreed to be a sounding board for our son as he considered alternative opportunities. That's the kind of kid my son is. He makes special connections with people, and it speaks volumes for his coach also.

We are lucky parents whose son insisted from about sixteen years old that he take the lead in all communications and interactions with coaches. My husband and I stay the hell out of the baseball. It's our son's career and connections, and we are very proud that he takes on this adult responsibility. We view our roles as trusted mentors and advisors. We do our homework, and we pay the bills because the cost is impossible for a young man to bankroll. Heck, it's been hard for us all along. Within two weeks of getting cut, we again traveled the country at considerable expense, looking at some of the college baseball programs interested in him as a player. We reached out to our college advisor who helped us place our son out of high school and received some help, but time was just too short. It's hard to gauge whether you're going to be a good match with a program when the coaches and players are in a rush. With the draft being in late July, one coach told our son he was only interested if his starting position player went in the draft. Our son noted that he could not wait that long though he sincerely appreciated the coach's candidness.

Coaches who took new jobs at different schools were the most frantic and inconsistent with regards to communicating with and interviewing our son as a prospective player. Coaches would reach out and act interested, only to go silent or to wait several weeks before picking up the ball again as if they never went silent. We visited one school where the head coach of an elite program had not bothered to watch online footage of our son playing. There was plenty of current footage out there. Imagine. He spent a whole day wasting everyone's time and money when he hadn't done his most basic homework. This caught us off guard. We saw that the rush we felt was like what the coaches were experiencing. In some ways the coaches seemed even more frantic. It was clear that many coaches relied solely on other coaches' recommendations. While that is a vital component, it would probably be best to spend five minutes watching a prospective player to confirm interest. What we all saw was that coaches were reacting as we were to a new recruiting landscape, experiencing the chaos of a paradigm shift they were swiftly learning to navigate for the best odds.

After our son was cut, I followed trends in the Transfer Portal closely. Many college coaches from elite programs were now making heavy use of the Transfer Portal to both recruit and cut players. High school players were no longer in high demand the way they once were. Overnight, the cycle of college recruiting seemed to go from expecting a baseball player to be in college for three to four years, to expecting a meager one to two years. I will emphasize here that it takes four years to complete college. Some types of brain development can't be rushed. Academic development and critical thinking skills develop over time. The four-year college experience is grossly out-of-sync with the new college baseball player—a just-in-time, plug-and-play commodity. Freshmen college baseball players are primarily in an extended try-out for the team. There is no commitment to the baseball player or their stable academic progress towards a college degree. That basic expectation is a thing of the past; it's a one-year try-out. It's a holding pen while coaches compare the players, they have to the players they can get from other programs via the Transfer Portal to, lastly, incoming high school recruits. (Honestly, if your son is an elite enough player to go in the draft out of high school, they might be better off going in the draft right now because of the turbulence in college baseball. Your son might end up sitting on the bench behind a twenty-four-year-old man who's been playing collegiate baseball for six years.)

In my efforts to understand the paradigm shifts my son got caught in, I paid attention to the college baseball media surrounding the Transfer Portal. Baseball America, D1 Baseball, and others were all atwitter about the latest star player to be poached from another elite program. There was casual mention of the numbers of players entering the Transfer Portal and lots of speculation about the college destinations of the high performing elite college players. But there was no critical analysis other than hype about the stars and the excitement the chaos brought. Nobody was talking about forcing players (and large numbers of players!) into the Transfer Portal. Nobody was talking about what was going to happen to the players stuck in the Portal with no college interest.

College baseball mass media exists to make money and to promote the sport, college, team, coaches, and star players. It's about manufacturing excitement and engagement for your eyeballs, and it's uncritical. There is little thoughtful reflection on the sport or trends. I had to research long and hard to find articles and commentary that didn't hype the Transfer Portal. I listened to many coaches talk about the Transfer Portal and whether they used it to recruit players. Coaches who didn't like excessive Portal use referred to it is as "free agency." Not one coach over the many I listened to over the summer directly discussed what they heavily use the Transfer Portal for: cutting players and cutting large numbers of players. Euphemisms by coaches were used such as "we had to make the numbers come out," or "players leave for more playing time," or "the Transfer Portal works like it always has." I believe the lack of frankness on behalf of the coaches is due to the possibility that it will hurt recruiting. Coaches wouldn't want families to fully understand how they are using the Transfer Portal because "high risk" doesn't help them recruit. Coaches want you to feel confident that your son has a real shot at playing time.

I also wonder about ethical coaches sensing a great wrong to many players. I wondered if there was unease with the paradigm shifts in recruiting and its effects on young college players—teenagers really. A family whose son was cut from a team doesn't want to discuss or disclose this fact for obvious reasons. It's a blow like none other. It is a huge setback in both academics and playing career, not to mention the emotional toll it takes. With social media it's also highly public information. (According to the NCAA, only coaches and admins have access to the Transfer Portal, but the baseball media seems to have easy access to names and stats.) Remember that prospective coaches rely heavily on the previous coach's recommendations. It's simply good business for cut players and their parents to keep their mouths shut and move along. The media might not want to discuss the large numbers of players being cut because it doesn't make for positive branding. To be fair, it also might be too early to write about the trends because they are still in flux. Twitter over the summer was also alight with plenty of criticism of college players who used the Portal to further their baseball careers by heading to a better team and conference. Other baseball fans mocked players who couldn't find another college program with the usual tropes: survival of the fittest, cream rises to the top, keep the big fish and throw the minnows back, and so on. On the one hand, that's true. But on the other ... if you aren't in a college baseball program that cuts large numbers of players, then you don't understand.

These players are not defective and entitled teenagers who can't be loyal to a program. Many of these players were forced into the Transfer Portal by their coaches because coaches now have easy access to players outside of their own college programs. And don't forget the bonanza created when the COVID eligibility rule gave an additional year to baseball players who were in college in 2020. Elite position players are in abundance right now. There are nine starting players per team. To access this bonanza of older, experienced Transfer Portal players, coaches must cut younger talent. Yes, the players technically have to choose to enter the Transfer Portal, but they aren't given a choice by their coaches. The NCAA conveniently doesn't keep track of why players enter the Portal. What would you do if you were a kid who was all-in on baseball and your coach said you must enter the Portal, or they will un-roster you? See? There is no choice. The Transfer Portal has been quickly commandeered by coaches to cut players for older, college-experienced men.

What I saw last summer in terms of a lack of thoughtful recruiting does not bode well for many young, elite student-athletes in the sport—especially players out of high school. Taking the time to get to know a player and make sure they are a match no longer seems to matter. Freshman year is a try-out. College baseball is becoming plug-and-play for a year or two for most players. Graduation rates? The culture of such programs and perhaps all of college baseball could be compromised, but will anyone take notice? The NCAA? For yuks I looked up the NCAA's Transfer Portal data for 2020 and 2021 D1 baseball (https://www.ncaa.org/sports/2022/4/25/transfer-portal-data-division-i-student-athlete-transfer-trends.aspx). I was pleased to see the NCAA tracking destinations of players who enter the Transfer Portal. Upon further study, I also saw what was missing from the stats and misleading.

The NCAA Transfer Portal statistical data is available from the years 2020 and 2021 and limits itself to NCAA stats. It doesn't track transfers to junior college or NAIA or drop-outs. First, it lists the number of D1 players who entered the Portal that year. Second, it lists the "Divisional Destination of NCAA Transfers" and graphs the proportions of transfer student-athletes who went to another NCAA D1, D2, or D3 school. The graph shows that 66% of transfers find another D1 college to play baseball at. This is misleading, because scrolling farther down I see that only 42% of D1 NCAA baseball players find another NCAA college to play at. That's less than half of all D1 baseball players who enter the Transfer Portal. Players who didn't or couldn't transfer to another NCAA baseball program are entirely left out of that first graph. What? That's entirely misleading.

The NCAA should include those discounted players in all statistics across the board. Truthfully, don't tell me it's all that hard to track players to NAIA, JUCO, dropouts, etc. *Just ask.* The NCAA stats page does not tell the whole story of the Transfer Portal effects, not by a long shot. Here's a more complete look at the outcomes.

2020–21 Transfer Portal Outcomes, NCAA D1 Baseball Student-Athletes

■ D1 ■ D2 ■ D3 ■ Withdrew from Portal ■ Still Exploring Options, Transferred to non-NCAA, or Left Sport

Still Exploring Options, Transferred to non-NCAA, or Left Sport 52% • D1 28% • D2 13% • Withdrew from Portal 6% • D3 1%

Overall, the NCAA's statistical data on the Transfer Portal is a mediocre, misleading first start, but it's a start! Here's what's missing from the NCAA statistics:

1. Add the "Unknown Destination" category of players into all statistics across the board with an explanation of where those players might have ended up. Do the research and find out who they are and where they went, whether they dropped out, etc., and add those stats.

2. The NCAA should be asking *why* a student is entering the Transfer Portal. Cut? Not a match with the school? Looking for a better opportunity? Make the stats public.

3. Survey players three months after they enter the Portal. Ask their destination. Make the stats public.

4. Survey players who remain in Portal after a calendar year. Ask their destination. Make the stats public.

5. Survey all players after six years. Make long term stats public.

6. Track graduation rates. Make the stats public.

7. Get serious about protecting NCAA private data. Why does the un-college-affiliated baseball media have access to private information that the public does not? Why is that private information all over social media? Make it all public or keep it private.

Solutions to the problems the Transfer Portal has introduced will have to be explored and resolved by those who are experts in the field. I do think coaches should have limits on the number of players they can cut. Coaches and colleges who cut large numbers of players should be held accountable to the players they cut in terms of money and support in finding another college program. These are young people we are talking about, and they made a huge commitment to the NCAA, a coach, and a college program. It costs *lots* of money and time and takes expertise to play at your college. Loyalty matters. Do a great job recruiting players for your college program. Make it worth a player's time to stay and be all at your college! Unintended consequences naturally ensue with any rule change—look at the turbulence the Transfer Portal has caused. The rule change was supposed to help undergraduate students-athletes find a college match without having to sit out a year if their first school didn't work out. The coaches primarily own it now.

I can appreciate that the NCAA has its hands full with all the changes in college sports. I believe that the business of college sports is incredibly difficult to balance with college players' interests. Those who are underage and not at the table lose out—look at those high school kids in 2020, who lost out to the COVID-extra-year college players. But seeing as how the players are the commodity being consumed, they will surely gain more of a voice over time. It's happening now and it's a good thing. Baseball is a great sport with a terrific college tradition. It's all of it … the good and the problematic. There can only be nine players on the field at a time. It's a reality that you must go where you can play, and where you are able to stay long enough to get a college degree. There are still plenty of coaches out there who put personal integrity and the development of young men at the center of their college baseball coaching jobs and aren't commandeering or won't commandeer the Transfer Portal at the expense of young men. These coaches are what we expected as the norm across the field before all the paradigm shifts. Most of these college programs don't tend to make the sports media news hype as often and are known for good solid baseball year in and year out. They produce MLB players regularly though not College World Series prospects annually. Thankfully, our son gravitated towards a stable, high-integrity program.

The college coaches who did not fully participate in the Transfer Portal bonanza and highly valued their jobs as educators of young men via the sport of college baseball took the time to engage thoughtfully and honestly with our son. We deeply appreciated hearing about those kinds of interactions and being part of some of those meaningful campus visits. Good, demanding coaches and stable programs are out there! Our son made a very wise choice in selecting his next college. It's one that his previous coach confirmed as a good choice given all the movement in college baseball presently. Our son chose a college program that has seen him for years, one that he seriously considered out of high school. They know him and he knows them. He knows the culture. This college does occasionally take players out of the Transfer Portal and some players transfer away, but it's a reasonable number—fewer than five players per year. The program is stable, and the players can focus on their academic careers as well as their baseball development. The coaches are emotionally intelligent, capable, and professional; they focus on the whole player. They have a sense of duty towards the young men they coach. It is college baseball as we expected it to be. It's still hard changing schools, moving to a different state, making new friends. He's starting all over again after just starting college. I'm also certain that our son will earn the playing time that another recruit was hoping for. The shock waves of the Transfer Portal will move throughout college baseball, but the basic trend is that there is more just-in-time talent available for the same number of spots on a team. There is and will be much more turbulence.

One last aside, my son is better off for having been a member of the program he started with his freshman year of college. He grew so much as a student and athlete. He developed by leaps and bounds. We continue to believe he was an excellent fit for the baseball program; he was simply a casualty of circumstance. We believe that many of the baseball players across the country in the Transfer Portal have been in a similar situation. The gut punch of getting cut will have its lessons also: Resilience, gratitude and grace-under-fire are terrific ingredients for a cup-is-half-full life and career. We could not be prouder parents of our honorable son and his passion for baseball, his teammates, his coaches, his college(s), his family, and his friends. Although our son's story is still in-progress we know it has a happy ending! I hope your son's story will have a happy ending also. To that end, take in all the information and advice Walter Beede shares in this book. Keep asking questions and do your homework so you can safely shepherd your children into programs where they will be challenged and thrive. Best of luck and Godspeed to our precious Boys of Summer!

THE SHIFT

INTRODUCTION

As I walked out of a local indoor baseball facility on a cold Saturday afternoon in January 2004, I faced an unexpected dilemma as a dad. My oldest son, Kyle, had just tried out for a travel baseball team and my youngest Tyler had tagged along to watch with me. At the time my boys were fourteen and twelve. This travel baseball world was brand new to all three of us. I only knew about it because I was a head college baseball coach. A colleague had given me a tip that many of the area's better high school baseball players were now playing travel baseball. I knew about leagues such as Babe Ruth and American Legion for high school–age athletes but had never heard of travel baseball. After the tryout was completed, a representative of the organization met with the athletes and their parents to discuss details. He was explaining the number of games and the time commitment required when he uttered a sentence that has been branded into my brain ever since. "Our program is for the best of the best that have a desire to play at the college level."

   That sentence struck a chord with me, but not for why you might think. As a dad, I immediately thought, "I am being sold something." I knew that team representative was adding perceived value. They were basically telling parents that they had the map and the knowledge to help athletes get onto college campuses to play baseball. Now my dilemma was that I grew up playing for the youth leagues. They did not cost much more than $100, and now I was being told that a year of baseball for Kyle would cost $3,000. What I did not know then but clearly do now is that business and youth baseball were about to become intertwined.

Many parents face this same dilemma that I faced back in 2004. How do we tell our sons, after they've heard a team representative say they are the path to college baseball, "sorry, you can't play for that team"? Year in and year out, parents find themselves faced with the same decision I had to make. We feel overwhelmed. What do we do if our athletes do not play travel baseball—are they left behind? Will they miss out on opportunities? As parents we most definitely want our children to be able to chase and live their dreams. Little boys and baseball go together; the dream has been around for over one hundred years. Heck it was mine; I wanted to play professional baseball.

On the ride home, both of my sons were excited about the workout and this new level of youth baseball. I didn't know then that helping them and other young men navigate this new world would become part of my life. I never envisioned our family spending summers traveling from Massachusetts to Georgia or California, or living in Louisiana to be closer to where they were playing. I didn't know that a decade later travel ball would be widely known as the place for college coaches and professional scouts to find quality, talented student-athletes, or that less than a decade after that it would be considered watered-down. Originally travel baseball was for high school-aged teenagers. Slowly it began to find its way to the younger age groups, starting as young as six years of age. A business that was started for the most part by young and entrepreneurial former college and professional players became a major industry. Many of these organizations today easily generate five hundred to seven hundred thousand dollars a year. What you may not realize is that many of the local and regional travel baseball programs in your area are now owned by massive investment groups that allow the original owner to still run the day-to-day operations. The business of youth baseball now has more in common with oil, pork bellies, citrus and other commodity businesses than many realize.

I also could not have imagined the changes at the top that would make all divisions and levels of college baseball much tougher and more exclusive. The many changes that I will discuss in this book will hopefully shed light on the new realities across the sport. These changes affect baseball from the Major League to Little League and every level in between. The industry of travel baseball does not want to inform or educate families or athletes about the rarity of success. And many families do not understand how minor league contraction, the reduction in the number of rounds in the MLB draft, an extra year of college eligibility due to COVID, and the NCAA transfer portal are creating a logjam on college baseball rosters.

So allow me, if you will, to take you on a quick journey through the world of youth baseball. My hope is that parents or possibly student-athletes gain valuable insight and a better understanding of where the game is currently, and in what direction it is headed. I would like parents and student-athletes to understand that the journey during childhood is far more important than the destination. We'll start back when a little boy with a bike, a bat, and a glove began his journey, one that would eventually lead to helping other little boys live their dreams within baseball.

THE WAY IT WAS FOR ME

Back in the day when a young boy played pickup baseball at the neighborhood sandlot or local Little League field, it was simply a time with friends and classmates. We'd ride our bikes to those fields with a glove stuck on one hand grip and our bats held across the handlebars. The excitement and anticipation of practicing and playing games raced through our hearts. Little League was a dream. Playing for a team and wearing a uniform that bore a MLB team's name? It didn't get better. I played for the Wyoma Senators and the Wyoma Dodgers. Those years from age nine through fifteen were simply magical. All the hits and defensive plays, as well as strikeouts and errors, were such a magical time in our lives. We played against younger and older friends from surrounding schools and neighborhoods. To this day, I remember the names, the games, and the scores. They are forever ingrained in my memory. And when life presents an opportunity to spend time with old friends, often we drift into banter and stories from days past. The glory days are what some refer to them as, but for me they are part of the foundation of who I would become as a player, coach, and most of all a father.

They say that having a good memory should be considered a blessing. I remember days as well as moments. I literally see faces and events when I think back. As far as my baseball career was concerned, May 19,1978, was the moment that my path within the game changed. It was a Friday in Lynn, Massachusetts, at a junior high school game during my ninth-grade year. Back in those days, junior high was seventh through ninth grade. Up until this day, I was considered a fringe to an average baseball player. I had never made an all-star team. For the most part, prior to 1978, when I was fifteen years old, I never felt I would play beyond high school—if I even was able to make the vaunted Lynn English varsity baseball team.

The day was an extremely chilly and blustery one on that field by the Atlantic Ocean. My team, the Pickering Junior High Tigers, was trailing Corbett Junior High 5-2 in the top of the sixth inning when I came to the plate with two outs and the bases loaded. A cold, bone-chilling wind was blowing off the ocean toward home plate, right into my face. My hands were red and raw. The Corbett pitcher had one pitch and he only needed one pitch, because even at that young age he was throwing a ninety mile per hour fastball that none of us could see, let alone hit. As you might imagine he was a bit wild, which is what led to those two runs and the runners who were on base as I stepped in the box.

Now they tell me the ball traveled a substantial distance over the fence, but when I swung and made contact, I simply put my head down and sprinted towards first base. I never tracked the flight of the baseball. In hindsight I wish I had, as it turned out it would be the very first homerun of my young baseball career. As I rounded second base, I saw the umpire with his hand in the air and then looked at my stunned teammates lining up at home plate. I remember at that exact moment thinking maybe—just maybe—I might be able to make the Lynn English team after all.

In the summer of 1978, my father was offered a new job in the central part of Massachusetts, in a city called Fitchburg. It's a place known for its paper mills and for being part of the oldest football rivalry in the country, versus crosstown rival Leominster. My dream of becoming a Lynn English Bulldog would not come to fruition. Instead, I now found myself in a new city and new high school. A new school meant new teammates and friends. It was a big adjustment for a fifteen-year-old.

During my sophomore year at my new school, I met an upperclassman named Mike Cormier, a starting pitcher who invited me to an off-season workout at a local elementary school. As I walked into the gymnasium with Mike, several other upperclassmen and head coach Mike Bourque welcomed me to the team. Now in those days, high school consisted of sophomores, juniors, and seniors. To play a varsity sport as a sophomore would be a huge accomplishment but being a new student at a new school in a new city would make this more of a challenge. As the upperclassmen began to get loose, coach Bourque asked me where I was from and a little about my baseball background. As I was telling him where I was from and how I ended up at the workout, the upperclassmen decided they were going to put me to the test right away. They had set the team's Jugs machine to a speed of one-hundred miles per hour with tennis balls screaming towards home plate. They then told me, "Okay Mr. Lynn, why don't you show us who you are."

As I stepped up the hastily set up home plate area, I put my helmet on and grabbed a team-issued Tennessee Thumper aluminum bat. I could feel the eyes of all in the gym suddenly shift to me, the new guy. As I watched the first couple tennis balls flash before me, I settled in and prepared to attempt to hit a few of these green colored lasers. I fouled the first few tennis balls off, which in and of itself was a great accomplishment. I then started to hit balls all over the gym with authority. Much to the upperclassmen's amazement—as well as coach Bourque's—I could make consistent contact. From that day forward, I felt as if I might have a legitimate chance of making the Fitchburg High varsity team.

And make it I did. On Monday, April 2, 1979, I found myself in the opening day starting lineup versus Monty Tech High School. Starting as a sophomore made my dad beam with pride, knowing the odds I had overcome to make myself known in a new city at a new school. Over the next three years, I would go on to start and play every inning of every game at Fitchburg High. During the summers of my sophomore and junior years I played on the Gardner American Legion Post 129 team. Making an American Legion team in the late 1970s and early 1980s was a great accomplishment. Post 129 was a collection of student-athletes from four area high school programs. Over seventy athletes tried out for eighteen roster spots. After I made the Gardner legion team as a sophomore, I began to face much higher-level talent and competition. In fact, in my first year of American Legion I found myself squaring off with future MLB first-round draft pick and big leaguer Ron Darling. Several MLB scouts were there to watch Ronnie pitch. He was a freshman at Yale at the time, nineteen years old versus my sixteen years. I did not know it then, but it was this game that put my name into the book for area MLB scouts. That day, I would say, was pretty good: three-for-four with a home run off the future New York Mets star.

At the completion of my senior year of high school, a local MLB scout named Lennie Merullo came by my house a few days prior to the yearly MLB amateur draft. It was at this time that I learned I might be a draft selection. I already had a scholarship opportunity at Arizona State University. ASU head coach Jim Brock had never seen me play, but he had access to MLB scouting reports and had offered me a scholarship during my senior year. At the time, the then-named PAC-10 was the premier college baseball conference in the country. It was comparable to what the Southeastern Conference (SEC) is in today's baseball landscape. While listening to Mr. Merullo speak, I distinctly remember thinking "There is no way I am getting drafted," but I was honored that he was having me fill out paperwork that allowed me to be a part of the draft.

On Saturday June 6, 1981, I graduated high school. While the rest of my classmates attended a yearly tradition known as Beach Week, I stayed behind—just in case a phone call came during the MLB draft scheduled for June 8–10. In the days of no cell phones or beepers, I knew that if I was drafted, I would receive a phone call or a Western Union. Now that tells how old I am, as many student-athletes may not even know what a Western Union telegram is. I guess we could call it the email process before there was the internet. As luck would have it, a phone call came on June 10 at 9:11 am. It was Mr. Merullo telling me I had been selected in the thirteenth round of the MLB draft. In what would alter my life in more ways than I could have ever imagined, I decided to forgo my scholarship to ASU and sign with the Chicago Cubs. When I did, Mr. Merullo uttered words that would forever be etched in my soul: "You will now attend the college of baseball in Mesa, AZ, and learn to be a big leaguer."

Those words would haunt me for over forty years, as my experience as a minor league player was not long lasting. The year I was drafted by the Cubs, the team was sold. There was new ownership and new management, and in a case of out with the old and in with the new, I was shown the door during the spring of 1982. After not even a full year of opportunity, playing one game a week for twelve weeks, I learned my first life lesson: never make any decision based on money.

Now many might think I could simply join my classmates as a freshman in college, but that was not the case. I was no longer eligible for a college scholarship because I had signed a professional contract. On my own since my father had passed away during my junior year in high school, I had to work and pay bills. In those days there were not the independent professional leagues that exist today. The only college summer league was the Cape Cod league, and as the name states it was for college athletes. I unfortunately was on the outside looking in. Over the next ten years, I played on semiprofessional teams in the Stan Musial league in hopes of catching scouts' attention and being able to sign as a free agent. Although I continued to play at a high level, that opportunity never transpired. After I was too old to be scouted, I kept playing because I love the game. From 1982 to 1997 I played for the Lunenburg Phillies and Shrewsbury Colt 45's. I also began helping at the area high school, Auburn High, as an assistant varsity coach.

My sons were born in the early 1990s—Kyle on November 14,1990, and Tyler on May 23, 1993. On the day Tyler was born, a

Sunday, I had a 10:00 a.m. game in Milford, MA. I played that day and had two triples and a base hit. We won, and the next morning the Worcester Telegram and Gazette had Tyler's name in the box score as a new arrival! I was extremely excited as a new father to be able to share my love and passion for the sport of baseball with my sons. I dreamt of watching them play little league someday and being able to watch them from the stands. When they turned nine and seven years of age, I was offered the opportunity to become an NCAA Division III head baseball coach. My boys joined me at practices and games during my tenure. They even participated in many of the practices. They loved being around older players and learned many of their basic skills within the game by watching, emulating, and then implementing them into their own bodies. Even at their young ages, I could see in their eyes the inner passion beginning to build for the sport of baseball.

In my early years as a college coach, while out recruiting several local American Legion and Senior Babe Ruth tournaments, I began to hear about these "AAU" travel baseball tournaments. This was truly the very beginning of hearing that term, *travel baseball*. I was told these teams were made up of the best players from all over New England. As I began to scout and evaluate athletes at these various tournaments, it was clear they were. Attending travel baseball tournaments suddenly became part of my recruiting. As both a college head coach and a father, I could see my sons were going to be exposed to a different path than I had been. What I did not know is that events were already taking place that would make their baseball journeys, and the journeys of so many millions of boys, radically different than the one I experienced.

THE EARLY YEARS OF TRAVEL BALL

When I became a father in the early '90s, I looked forward to sharing my love and passion for the sport of baseball with my sons Kyle and Tyler. When they were young, we played catch in the backyard. The boys tagged along with me as I coached at the high school and college levels. Soon it was their turn to play little league. Neither of my boys had ever heard of or played travel baseball. Instead, they played Wiffle ball and local pickup games in the neighborhood, or they rode their bikes to a local field. Their experience up until then wasn't much different than mine had been.

When Kyle became a teenager, a few local travel coaches approached me about his interest in playing for them. If you're not involved in baseball, you may be wondering what a travel ball program is. In a nutshell, travel baseball is just what it sounds like—teams roving around different states or cities to play baseball against other teams. It came about because Little League and other recreational leagues (or rec leagues) were considered weaker in caliber. Travel baseball was created to be more advanced and serious. Overall, these teams included only elite-level participants and had an independent coach whose main aim was helping the players go as far as they could in the game. Everything within the world of travel baseball is often promoted as better, including the players, the coaches, and the experiences. The overall perception is that travel baseball is more intense as well as more rewarding.

In the northeast, travel baseball teams initially were geared more toward the junior high or middle school age group. Legendary Massachusetts high school coach Frank Niles, whom I played against in our semi pro days, spoke with me about what travel baseball was like in that era. Frank started the South Shore Baseball Club in Hingham, MA, in 1989. Back then it was more of a social club for baseball. They had memberships, clinics, camps, and year-round indoor and outdoor training. However, they had no teams. "Our best players were starting to drift and go try out for these teams, the New England Mariners then the Mass Lightning. So, after about four years of seeing that happen, the demand was there for us to do a similar thing. So, we started the South Shore Seadogs." With so few teams in existence, recruiting was regional. The Sea Dogs attracted "kids from Cape Cod, New Hampshire, or Rhode Island." It was an honor to get a tryout invite from the Sea Dogs. "We had a fifteen-year-old team that won a national invitational tournament in Kingsport, Tennessee," recalls Frank. That team included Jason Delaney, who played six seasons in the minors and was inducted into the Boston College athletics hall of fame in 2022. They were well coached and talented.

Down the east coast, in New Jersey, Joe Barth Jr. was in the early years of the Tri State Arsenal program. Joe grew up in the game. His father coached the American Legion Post 72 team for decades. Joe took over head coaching in 1981 and won the American Legion World Series in 1991. He was aware of other travel teams being formed, but at the time he was working with hitters and running camps. The parents of the student-athletes he worked with are the ones who encouraged him to start a travel team. "[I] decided if I was going to do it, I was going to do it right … In the early days of travel baseball when we were hundreds of miles away playing, everybody we would play against had a good team. The kids knew they had to compete in each game. It was truly exceptional baseball."

Despite travel baseball's good reputation, I didn't mention the coaches' interest with Kyle. It was after one of my team's practices in February 2004 that he brought it up on his own. My sons and I were playing catch inside the college's gym, and Kyle mentioned a travel team was having a tryout he might want to attend. I felt if this was something Kyle wanted to try, I would explore what the team and program were all about. So, now fully engaged in Dad mode, I took Kyle to his first travel ball tryout. My youngest, Tyler, tagged along to watch. It was an indoor tryout. About fifty student-athletes and their parents hung on every word the program director uttered. He explained the time commitment—the demand on each family's time during the spring and summer seasons. There would be no opportunity to play at the local and travel levels together; it was one or the other. Then, just before the athletes were put through their paces, the director laid out the costs: tryout fees, practice costs, yearly team fees. Let's just say that at that very moment my calculator mind sprang into action.

As the talk concluded, Tyler and I sat back to watch Kyle. The first event was a timed sprint with players paired together. Kyle and I were not fleet of foot, so this was not his strength. As they progressed into the fielding drills and workouts, Kyle began to flash a family strength, his arm. Kyle was blessed with a cannon strapped to his right shoulder. I noticed the director walk over and say something to Kyle, who pointed me out to him. The director walked over to me and introduced himself. As he began to tell me about how his program really needed a catcher in the fourteen-year-old age group, I explained to him that as a college coach my summers were spent being a dad as well as a recruiting coordinator. It would be difficult for me to fit in. However, I could clearly see there were quality athletes trying out, and I would discuss with Kyle whether this was something he wanted to dedicate his summer to.

When the workout ended, I could see on my son's face his excitement and confidence in his performance. As the three of us drove home, I began to ask Kyle how he felt about not being able to play with his friends from school or possibly missing summer basketball. We began to discuss what the commitment meant for him and the upcoming summer season. From the backseat came a comment, "I really want to play for that team" Tyler had clearly put his vote front and center. When I asked him why, he stated, "I can play basketball in the winter, and I want to play baseball in high school." This is where my sons had different mindsets. Kyle was a homebody with his buddies and enjoyed being a part of the group; Tyler was driven to try new things and challenge himself in the way he saw my college teamwork out.

After we got home, Kyle decided to wait another year for travel baseball. He'd enjoy his summer baseball and basketball seasons with his friends from school. Upon further research I discovered the additional costs as well as time commitments that travel baseball required, such as travel, meals, weekends of doubleheaders, and three-day tournaments. I gave Kyle the option of playing travel baseball or American Legion; he chose to play with friends and classmates on the local Legion team.

As good as travel ball was in the northeast, it developed later and more slowly than in the south and on the west coast. One of the first travel baseball organizations to start the trend of offering amateur athletes an opportunity to compete versus teams from around the country was East Cobb Baseball in Marietta, Georgia. It's founder, Guerry Baldwin, wanted an option for the children and families who wanted a more advanced caliber of baseball. His first team was comprised mostly of players from the Marietta team that won the 1983 Little League World Series. They went on to win the 1985 Pony League World Series, 1986 Babe Ruth Baseball 13–15 World Series, and 1988 Babe Ruth Baseball 16–18 World Series. Baldwin moved to full travel ball in the 1990s. Along the way, the thirty-acre East Cobb Baseball Complex was built: eight fields, indoor and outdoor batting cages, meeting rooms, covered dugouts, and living quarters for out-of-town players and their families.

On the West Coast, Rob Bruno founded the NorCal Baseball Club in 1992. Back then, he started off with just one 15U team— which won the AAU 15U National Championship. Motivated by the team's success, NorCal began selecting players for junior, sophomore, and freshman teams. (Rather than group players by age, NorCal groups them by graduating year.) Those early years were anchored by players like Pat Burrell, Jimmy Rollins, Xavier Nady, and Dontrelle Willis. On its website, NorCal states "It is our mission to create an environment for young athletes to achieve their dreams of playing college and professional baseball. We also believe that through the game of baseball we can help build character and determination that will be an asset to our players not only for the game of baseball but for life." Truth be told, the organization has given the baseball world some tremendous players. They've created a legacy and have set benchmarks for young, aspiring baseball athletes.

Other early, nationally known teams were the Orlando Scorpions, founded by Sal Lombardo in 1994; the Banditos Baseball Club, founded by Ray DeLeon in 1996; and Dirtbags Baseball, founded by Andy Partin in 2002. These teams needed places to play, and they found them in the showcases and tournaments run by another organization, Perfect Game. Started by Jerry Ford in 1993, by 1997 they were hosting tournaments nationwide. As a college coach, I became fascinated with the information on older student-athletes that was available on the Perfect Game website. Rankings were broken down state by state as well as nationally. The profiles provided skill set information such as velocity, a scouting grade from 1–10, and most importantly contact information. This information was fantastic, as I could now reach out to student-athletes all around the new England region. As an NCAA D3 head coach, I felt this truly opened access to athletes that I may not have had the ability to see or stumble across at a tournament or ballpark. But I wondered how they were able to rank athletes from every state. Where did they evaluate these athletes and who was evaluating them? I soon put the pieces together of how travel baseball and perfect game were intertwined. To be ranked, players had to attend a tournament or showcase conducted by Perfect Game. According to an October 2018 article on their website, "this was all about getting the best kids together to compete against one another so that PG could establish its player database and move forward with ranking the top prospects."

From 2004 to 2006, the interest in travel baseball had grown into a national phenomenon. Suddenly the number of travel baseball teams in our area had grown from a handful to well over fifty teams within an hour's drive of us in central Massachusetts. Teams from Connecticut, Rhode Island, and Massachusetts were reaching out to me in hopes of my youngest son, Tyler, try out. Or they outright offered a roster spot. At the time he was an eighth grader and eligible to play American Legion baseball. I felt strongly that Tyler would benefit more by joining Kyle on the local Legion team. It ended up being a great season for both the boys, as they were able to play "big boy" baseball together for the first time!

The following year, when Tyler joined Kyle at Auburn High School, the world of travel baseball was in full blown recruiting mode. Suddenly there were so many teams throughout the New England area, and they were all calling to inquire about my sons. I was told by these program owners how inferior local Legion baseball was compared to national travel baseball and tournaments held in the greater Atlanta, GA, area. Now I was what I would call a knowledgeable baseball man, but I felt that as a father I needed to do some homework on this topic. I began to look on the internet for answers. I learned of a yearly event held each summer in East Cobb, GA, home of Geurry Baldwin's East Cobb Baseball. It seemed that Perfect Game founder Jerry Ford and Guerry Baldwin had come to an agreement where Perfect Game would use the East Cobb complex as the home of a yearly tournament for 14U–17U athletes. Word began to spread. In those days a team truly needed to show that they were elite. Teams had to state the names on the rosters to see if those players were in demand from college coaches and MLB scouts. College coaches from all over the country would make the yearly trek to East Cobb, Georgia to see the best baseball players from all over the country. As word began to spread that many high-level recruits and potential MLB draft picks were attending Perfect Game events as high school freshman, sophomores, and juniors, suddenly travel teams were competing—and dare I say, recruiting—for the better players.

The first travel team Tyler played for was Team Connecticut as a fourteen-year-old. It was compromised of twenty fourteen-year-old athletes from MA and CT. The schedule was regional with one national tournament held in Sarasota, Florida. When we arrived in Sarasota, I was absolutely stunned at the sheer number of teams from across the country. Tyler's team even played a team with Cal Ripken's son Ryan on it! There were over 500 teams that attended this five-day tournament. It was at this point that I started to think this was *much* bigger than I had ever imagined. As a college head coach with an extremely limited recruiting budget, I could understand why these events were drawing so many college coaches from around the country. Instead of a coaching staff having to fly to single games, they now could fly into these types of events and could scout student-athletes from their region or from across the country. Not only was it a significant cost saving for college programs, but it truly allowed a coaching staff to evaluate a student-athlete over a series of games as opposed to just one game.

Over Tyler's high school years, he would move on to play with a national team known at the time as the Virginia Canes. He would join this team after the completion of his high school season in early June and play until the end of July. During his time with the Canes, his team would win back-to-back Perfect Game National Championships. Those teams had players literally from all over the country: California, North and South Carolina, Virginia, and of course Massachusetts. It truly opened not only my eyes but Tyler's as well. Suddenly he went from the big fish in a small pond to an ocean of great players whom he played with and most importantly against.

When I talk with families about travel ball, there are positives that I cover. There's the greater competition. Your child's desire to compete at a higher level will encourage them to develop their own skills. Coaches of travel baseball typically have better connections, knowledge, and qualifications. Teams frequently employ former professional coaches at the highest levels of travel ball. The high-level tournaments give student-athletes opportunities for exposure to college coaches and professional scouts. Players get used to travel, which is what awaits them at the college and professional levels. They will experience steady growth if you select the right organization. A solid framework and curriculum underpin the practices, allowing for practical instruction and high-quality reps. There's the character development piece. Being on time, giving your all, and having a positive attitude are more influential on travel teams because they are more serious. Finally, there is the opportunity to play more games than rec league teams do.

It was during his travel ball years that Tyler's skill set truly blossomed. Being able to see the game at that speed allowed him to prepare his body and mind for that level of competition. In those days, travel baseball was truly for the talented players from across the country to gain exposure as well as an awareness of what the game at the college level and beyond would look like. There is no doubt in my mind that Tyler benefited a great deal not only from the team that he played on, but also the teams he played against. In my opinion this was the pinnacle of youth travel baseball. The competition was consistent, and the quality of baseball was truly of a high level.

WHAT ONCE WAS WILL NEVER BE

During the early years of travel baseball, 2000–2015, student-athletes and their families were truly getting a maximum return on their time and resources. The mission statement foremost of these programs was to allow similar caliber student-athletes to compete against each other on both a regional as well as national basis. Many of the original national programs truly had created an athletic environment that college coaches and MLB scouts felt was above average to elite competition. For those fifteen years, it was not uncommon to see hundreds of scouts and coaches at tournaments and showcases around the country. The talent level for many higher end national programs was the cream of the crop. Players from the east coast could now compete with programs from across the country.

I vividly remember being in East Cobb, GA, in July of 2009 for a 17U game that featured California's ABD versus a Southeast powerhouse Marucci Elite from Louisiana. Both programs featured elite NCAA D1 recruits and future MLB draft selections, including future NL MVP Christian Yelich on ABD. I was there as a dad, watching this game before Tyler's team the Canes played. What I vividly remember are the discussions among MLB scouts. They were so thrilled that they were able to see these two high level programs competing against each other as it allowed them to truly scout skill sets in such a competitive environment. For the decades prior to the year 2000, scouts and college coaches would only get to see these types of games in a national Connie Mack or American Legion series. Those games would never truly allow coaches or scouts access to the elite versus elite because they would only see one team from each part of the country. With the creation of national travel baseball programs, these coaches and scouts were now given front row seats to the country's best baseball players during the summer and fall. This ensured that student-athletes could be fully scouted and evaluated versus high levels of competition, which gave both college coaches and scouts a better understanding of how an athlete's skill sets would play at the higher levels.

Now during this game, the power of Twitter was in its infancy, so not much information was relayed across the country. But it was an absolute gem of a 16U game. Both starting pitchers were future MLB draft picks—Peter Tago for ABD and Ryan Eades for Marucci. The backstop was filled with college coaches and scouts with radar guns held in the air gathering information on every pitch. As each pitch was thrown, recorded, and evaluated, it was clear to me as both a former college coach and most importantly as a dad that this was *the* place to be if you were a high school–aged baseball player aspiring to play at the game's higher levels.

During the 16U WWBA (World Wood Bat Association) National Championship held that year, 2009, I watched over twenty games both with Tyler as a fan and when he participated with his Canes National team. It was very clear to me as a talent evaluator that the platform of Perfect Game was indeed a great opportunity for my son, as it was for all the student-athletes who were seeking opportunities to play beyond high school. The East Cobb complex had five big diamonds as well as baseball cages that allowed for teams to take batting practice before games. For someone like myself, a lifelong baseball junkie, this facility had it all. At every game being played stood the who's who of college coaches: University of Oregon, Louisiana State, University of Virginia, Georgia, South Carolina, North Carolina, Vanderbilt. MLB scouts were not only behind the backstop but also along the right and left field lines. This was truly the place where baseball's highest-level coaches and scouts wanted to be.

To give you an idea of how big of a deal these events had become, the Boras Corporation—yes, the agency of Scott Boras—had talent evaluators all over this event hoping to find the next big bonus baby that they could represent. It was not uncommon for an advisor from an agency to give parents a card in hopes of developing a relationship with these athletes and families. All of it is with the hope that these advisors could become players' agents in the future. They would collect student-athletes much like little kids collect Easter eggs. Agents receive five percent of a drafted player's signing bonus; many of the larger agencies represent anywhere from a few to as many as twenty players each draft. Each year after the draft, many agents can have clients that sign for anywhere from $1 million to as high as $10 million collectively, all with a healthy five percent representation fee. As you can see with this example, there is *lots* of money within the business of baseball.

This was Tyler's first experience on the national stage. I was a strong proponent of the American Legion program and was somewhat apprehensive about bringing Tyler to this event due to a lack of understanding of its significance. This particular week in Georgia proved to be a turning point in Tyler's young career. For the very first time, Tyler was not a big fish. In fact, Tyler played very sparingly. While his Canes team would go on to win the WWBA 16U National Championship, Tyler would only play one and a third innings. As we drove from Marietta, GA, back to Auburn, MA, I fully expected Tyler to ask me about his lack of opportunity during the week. I was shocked to hear him say to me, "Dad, now I know what it looks like and what I need to work on." He came away from that week knowing what the talent across the country looked like and what he would need to do to find his way within the game at the college level.

One month later, as an alternate for the prestigious Area Code games, Tyler's baseball future would take a dramatic turn. Most Area Code rosters are filled with rising seniors in high school. Tyler had just completed his sophomore year of high school and had been selected as an alternate pitcher in case of injury. As luck would have it, Tyler was asked to pitch in one of the early games during the 2009 Area Code games. This yearly event is the summer's biggest event. Rosters for the Area Codes are selected by MLB scouts. Tryouts are held each year in June and the event at the time was held in Long Beach, California, in early August.

Now, it is one thing to make an Area Code roster. It is a much different dynamic to pitch in this event as a sophomore. When we arrived in Long Beach, CA, Matt Hyde the manager for the New York Yankees Area Code team informed Tyler that there had been a few changes on the Yankees roster for the event. Now I could see Tyler speaking with Matt down on the field as the team was preparing to get loose for a pre-tournament workout. As I made my way to find a seat in the stadium to watch the team workout, a former minor league teammate, Bruce Seid, walked over to me. "Man, they let anyone in these events," he exclaimed. I had not seen Bruce since spring training with the Chicago Cubs in 1983. We shook hands and gave each other a hug, and Bruce told me that he was now the scouting director for the Milwaukee Brewers. That is a very high-level position within professional baseball. While catching up with Bruce, Tyler tapped me on the shoulder. He was smiling from ear to ear as he told me in front of Bruce, "I was asked to pitch against the vaunted Milwaukee Brewers So Cal team. Coach Hyde just told me that I was not only on the roster, but he wanted to know if my arm felt good enough to pitch tomorrow." I introduced Bruce and Tyler, and while shaking my son's hand, Bruce said "that roster is loaded, looking forward to watching you pitch." The Brewers Area Code roster was littered with future MLB draft selections which included a strong group of standout players, such as Tony Wolters, Christian Lopes, Travis Harrison, and Austin Wilson. Many members of their pitching staff would go on to pitch at the MLB level: Aaron Sanchez, Peter Tago, and Adam Plutko. Prior to this game, Tyler was not ranked and not considered a high-level college prospect by any major college. But that would change dramatically after this Area Code event.

I had never attended an Area Code event before either as an athlete or coach and had no idea what to expect. For Tyler and I this was an entirely new environment. When we walked into Blair Field, we both stopped in our tracks. The entire backstop area was filled with scouts, radar guns, cameras, and video equipment set up on tripods. Not only the backstop area but the left and right field seats were jam packed with college coaches, agents, and MLB executives. Instantly we both looked at each other as we had absolutely no idea the magnitude of this event. We were not in Auburn, MA, anymore! Tyler made his way down to the dugout area, and I walked up to the top row on the first base side of the field, trying to find a quiet spot to watch the game. My adrenaline was racing as I found a seat.

Suddenly, Bruce spotted me in the sea of scouts and coaches and waved me over to sit with him. "Walt, what can you tell me about your son? What are we going to see out of him today?" I gave Bruce my "dad scouting report" and laughed. The game was tied 1-1 in the top of the third inning when Tyler jogged in from the left field bullpen. My heart was racing. Bruce, noticing my stern look, leaned over, and said, "It's only baseball, Captain, he'll be fine. He's a young kid facing an older line up, we all know that. Whatever happens, happens, so relax and enjoy this moment." Up until this event, Tyler had spent the entire spring and summer pitching anywhere from 84–88 miles per hour. What got Tyler on this team was his ability to throw his changeup in any count. It was an advanced swing-and-miss pitch. At his Area Code tryout, Scouts loved that pitch, so while his velocity was not where they wanted it, his ability to throw that changeup allowed him to be an alternate.

As Tyler watched the throw from the catcher go to second base, I could see him wipe his forehead that was dripping with sweat. The temperature at game time was a balmy 92 degrees. If I was nervous,

I could not imagine what Tyler was feeling. Bruce patted my back and uttered the words "and so it begins Walt" as Tyler delivered his first pitch. Now Bruce had his scouts down behind the backstop with a radar gun, and they were charting every pitch Tyler threw. The first batter Tyler faced he struck out, the next batter hit a ground ball to short, and the third hit a fly ball to centerfield. That earned me a comment from Bruce. "You holding out on me Walt? Your boy looks pretty good. How old is he?" When I responded with," He just turned sixteen," Bruce smiled and said, you' don't see many sixteen-year-olds throwing 90 to 93 with an advanced change up like that." My jaw dropped, "Did you say 90-93?"

Now if I could go back in time to that very moment, knowing what I know now, I would have elected to let Tyler maintain his childhood innocence. But from that one inning his life truly changed in a very big way. In this very moment my son would go from a happy go lucky young man to now having to carry the burden of expectation. I was taking a deep breath and looking around the lower half of the stadium after Tyler's first inning. Every single scout was writing notes. I mean literally, every scout's head was buried in their notepads writing. Suddenly there was a large shift by many coaches and MLB executives trying to squeeze into a seat behind home plate. As Tyler jogged out of the dugout to the mound for his second inning of work, I could tell he was much more relaxed. He was unaware at this point of his velocity, but he knew from his first inning of work that he could compete at this level. As Tyler proceeded to throw his final warm up pitches, Bruce leaned in and said, "This is the big boy part of the lineup. A few future MLB players coming up."

I was unfamiliar with these players as they were all from southern California. The first player to come to bat that inning was Cristian Lopes from Huntington Beach, CA. As Tyler threw a first pitch change up for a called strike, I notice a smile come to Christian's face. I think he may have felt like Tyler was getting cocky. The next pitch Tyler threw his changeup again as Christian swung as hard as he could to no avail. The next pitch Tyler threw was a hard, biting curve ball for a called third strike that got everyone's attention. On that third pitch, Tyler had just struck out one of the best high school hitters in the country and had now shown scouts his ability to throw three above average pitches. Suddenly I could see people pointing up in Bruce's direction, motioning him to come down to watch from their vantage point. Tyler again retired the side in order, and after two innings had three strikeouts and no hits allowed.

At this moment I noticed two gentlemen walking up my aisle; the taller one was looking right at me. He looked very familiar. As he got in front of me, the other gentleman asked "Mr. Beede?" "Yes sir, how can I help you?" I asked. "My name is Dan Evans"—former GM of the Dodgers—"and this guy might look familiar to you." It turns out the familiar looking man was two-time Cy Young award winner Brett Saberhagen. "Your son looks really good out there. We'd love to talk to you and Tyler after the game." I politely explained that I would like to wait until Tyler finished his outing and then we could chat. Now by this time as Tyler jogged out for his third and final inning of work, he was about to face the four-, five- and six-hole hitters for the Brewers. You might have heard of the four-hole hitter. His name was Christian Yelich. Tyler got him to ground out to second base and then struck out the next two hitters, both on nasty changeups. He pitched three shutout innings and more importantly his velocity had spiked to 90–93 mph. After this event, suddenly every college program from west to east was reaching out to Tyler. He also began to receive letters from MLB teams.

My point in telling you this story is to simply allow parents to understand that during a student-athlete's high school career, in the blink of an eye an athlete's future can be altered by one event. It cannot be pre-arranged; it cannot be scripted. I did not pay any money for Tyler's spot on that Area Code team. His lack of playing opportunities during his time on the 2009 Canes team did not negatively impact his future in any way. Allowing Tyler to experience the game at a higher level of play allowed him to see and feel what was needed to play at the higher levels of the sport. His physical preparation with Cressey Sports Performance during the winter of 2008, and the opportunity to be a part of the Canes National team, together created the foundation that allowed Tyler to have the confidence that he could indeed compete with and against the best athletes from across the country.

That summer was also my introduction to the financial struggle that can come with travel baseball. After the 2009 Area Code games in Long Beach, Tyler received an email congratulating him that he had been chosen for the Aflac All-American underclass team that was playing in San Diego in mid-August. This was truly an unexpected honor—and one that I had not prepared for. I was a single father working a 40-hour-a-week job and had barely just enough money for the Area Code event. Now Tyler was being invited to an additional showcase event that required a substantial amount of money for a five-day stay in San Diego. The economy was in a tough place in 2009, something many families today can relate to. I was living paycheck to paycheck and had not planned on an additional $1000 being spent on travel baseball. Tyler and I sat outside a Long Beach Starbucks so that we could use their Wi-Fi, and I put out an SOS to my friends via Facebook. I literally felt like a fool. But as a parent, I was between a rock and financial hard place. In that moment, I felt like I would let Tyler down if I didn't get him to San Diego. I could see in his face how much he wanted to attend this event. Fortunately, a friend, Rob Binnall, offered up his hotel points and rental car points. Without the help of Rob, that flight home would have been a challenge for me as a father.

In 2010, Tyler played in East Cobb with the Canes again. That summer was not only a memorable one, but an extremely expensive one. In a six-week span, we as a family had to travel to Georgia,

Florida, North Carolina, and California. The expenses were significant as we had to pay for hotels, airfare, food, gas, and entry fees. All totaled, the summer of 2010 turned out to cost over fifteen thousand dollars. Again, I had a decision to make as a dad, as I simply did not have that amount of money in savings. So, I used credit cards to make sure Tyler was able to attend. When I think back to the original tryout that Kyle attended back in 2004, never in my wildest dream would I have thought that I would be paying this amount of money for either of my sons to play youth baseball. As parents, we never want our children to be denied any opportunities while they are chasing their dreams. I was always aware of both Tyler's ability as well as the once-in-a-lifetime opportunities that he was being offered. He had earned them through his hard work and I wanted to make sure he was able to attend these events.

The one aspect of travel baseball (and all youth sports) that is not understood by parents at the early ages is the subliminal message of missing out. Travel baseball makes it clear that if you want your son to be the best and play with and against the best, it is going to be a commitment of both time and money. I had the background to understand Tyler's ability; no one had to tell me how good he was. As a baseball coach, I knew that the time and resources were going to help Tyler have a great experience as well as prepare him for the next levels of college and professional baseball. However, not every athlete will make it to this level and parents have to be honest with themselves as well as with their child. No amount of money can be spent to achieve that level of success; an athlete must have the talent, desire to succeed, and work ethic. A strong message for parents to remember is this: at sixteen, take your son to a college camp and ask the coaching staff to write you an honest evaluation of your son's current and projected skill sets. This is important for your child's future. If a college coach feels that your son has the ability to play in college, he will write it. If he feels that your son will not have that ability, then you will have decision. But at least you will have the truth.

Tyler's last year of travel baseball in 2010 would turn out to be an extremely memorable one. He was selected to play in many prestigious events and he now has great memories of his youth baseball experiences. Looking back, I can honestly say that for our family it was a great experience but an expensive one. The lessons that I learned, and continue to learn, I try to share with parents. Know who your son is as an athlete; do not leave that to others. Never be afraid of asking direct and tough questions. If your son is truly good enough, you will hear from college coaches and possibly MLB scouts. Never allow your fears of missing out, inferior competition, or being left behind be a driving force. Try to seek out an honest and direct evaluation of your son's ability before making any decisions that require a significant financial investment. Gather as much information as you can on your son's ability.

THE FEAR OF MISSING OUT

There is a false narrative in travel baseball that if student-athletes don't participate, they will be left behind. Do you remember the World Wood Bat Association game from 2009 that I mentioned? That 16U national championship didn't exist until 2005. The WWBA didn't exist until 1999. It is not a league or an association of member teams. The WWBA is an invention of Perfect Game. The idea was to have a high-quality, invite-only fall tournament. Limiting it to the best teams would attract college coaches and pro scouts. The promise of coaches and scouts attending would attract the best teams. And it worked. Perfect Game had developed a reputation for putting on good tournaments in East Cobb and elsewhere. That made travel team owners like East Cobb's Guerry Baldwin and Nor Cal's Rob Bruno willing to commit to a new fall tournament in Florida. What it developed into is now simply known as "Jupiter," after the city that hosts it.

By 2003, seventy-six teams were invited to Jupiter. That grew to eighty-five in 2010 and an even one hundred in 2022. Spread across five days and thirteen fields, the games commence in the morning at eight and typically don't end before ten o'clock at night. The event is so extraordinary, comprising so many highly regarded prospects, that the scouts and college coaches require golf carts to get from game to game quickly enough. It is largely recognized within the higher levels of baseball, meaning college coaches and MLB scouts, as the year's biggest and best event. To this day it is an invitation-only event. Its success is undeniable. It is also fair to say it got its start because travel organizations, college coaches, and scouts were sold on the fear of missing out. That fear does not just effect parents. College coaches and MLB scouts did not want to miss out on seeing student-athletes from across the country who would now be playing in one location over the course of five days. Travel organizations invited to Jupiter did not want to miss out on their athletes being seen.

The period of the early 2000s through 2015 was what I refer to as the first major shift in college recruiting and MLB scouting. Events like Jupiter offered a tremendous scouting and evaluation opportunity. Everyone wants to see athletes with their own eyes, and these big, national events offered college programs and professional organizations the opportunity to gather video and valuable information on how athletes compete versus better competition. Coaching staffs and scouts now had the ability to gather at one location a few times a year to see the country's best athletes. This solved many issues regarding recruiting budgets and scouting expenses. These events were also largely covered by all social media platforms. Parents and student-athletes now saw information in real time on their laptops and cell phones. This created an even bigger excitement level for both the participating athletes as well as those who wanted to take part in the future. Many student-athletes now were being evaluated and "picked apart" by real and make believe scouts. Make believe scouts are simply adults that want to offer their two cents on a player's ability—often times a parent who wants to see their son succeed and a peer fail. The weight of expectations for student-athletes during this period began to become very real. Rankings were now attached to a student-athlete and the pressure to live up to these rankings was extremely high. Parents need to understand that student-athletes have a bullseye on their backs once they are nationally ranked. If you take the time to look back at rankings from the early years of Perfect Game, there will be names that you remember. But most of those ranked athletes never found success at college or professional levels.

While the travel world of the mid 2000s and early 2010s can be seen as the glory days, today's travel baseball climate is much different. I think it is no coincidence that the emergence of social media platforms such as Facebook and the all-powerful Twitter began to have a massive impact on the travel baseball world. At events like Jupiter, suddenly every move was being reported around the country in 140-character increments. Interest grew and these tweets became must-view information. Words like velocity, foot speed, arm side run, exit velocity, and arm strength suddenly became part of the travel ball vocabulary. Rankings were being posted all over social media, both individual player rankings and rankings of travel teams in various age groups. Teams could now boast via post or tweet who played for them and where the team and players were ranked.

Suddenly all the summer tournaments and showcases had athletes and their families scurrying to their cell phones and laptops to see the event highlights. College coaches and MLB scouts purchased subscriptions so that they could see player evaluations written by Perfect Game staff. Elite alumni such as Buster Posey, Prince Fielder, Brandon Crawford, Nolan Arenado, Paul Goldschmidt, Garret Cole, and a host of other MLB players who'd played in Perfect Game events were hyped on PG's social media. What Perfect Game was telling all baseball families was that if a young athlete had dreams of playing college baseball or professional baseball, the road to those dreams went through Perfect Game.

In the early years of Perfect Game tournaments, it was challenging for teams to enter a national tournament. Teams had to demonstrate that they not only had talented athletes but that their teams could compete year in and year out with known, nationally prominent teams. Teams had to submit their rosters to Perfect Game staff members for them to decide if a team was allowed entry into their tournaments. Perfect Game knew that the quality of teams and athletes mattered a great deal to college coaches as well as MLB scouting staff. Perfect Game could afford to be selective because they had carefully created a platform that was in high demand. They held *the* events in July and October that every travel program in the country wanted to participate in. For travel programs, entry into these elite Perfect Game events became part of their marketing. Parents whose children weren't taking part felt like they might be missing out. As is the case when demand out grows supply, the greed of the sellers began to grow at an epic level.

I am certainly not going to paint a canvas with a broad brush and assume that every travel team operates in a certain way. Every single organization is different. The vast majority of travel baseball organizations at the older age levels play a significant role in the development of student-athletes. But some organizations started focusing less on player development and more on business development.

Finally, the ranking system that Perfect Game established for both teams and student-athletes caused families to be anxious and excited. A 1 meant the player was not college caliber. A 10 was a division 1 quality player. Obviously, parents wanted to have their children ranked and have articles written about them. The pressure on those who did not become part of ranked travel teams began to grow as they literally saw every day, everywhere on the internet that they were missing out. I feel it is important to remember that we are talking about highly impressionable young teenagers that were beginning to believe that they did not measure up to what they were reading on social media and the internet. As is the case with all children and teenagers there is a competitive feeling with trying to keep up with their peers locally as well as around the country. That competitive environment quickly spread to parents as well. Many parents felt that their student-athlete was as good or better than players that were now ranking within their state. Travel programs began to use this as fuel to get parents to believe that if their children played on these "elite" programs they would be seen by ranking services such as Perfect Game and PBR. Travel programs from across the country started spreading the word that they—and only they—could offer student-athletes better exposure, more skilled coaching, better experience, a stronger and more versatile skillset, and the opportunity for a college career or even the MLB draft.

It helped that around this same time, former travel ball players were ascending to major league rosters—Bryce Harper, Mike Trout, Mookie Betts, Francisco Lindor, and Garret Cole among them. Some travel baseball organizations used this to fuel the message that travel ball was the only way to baseball success. That, however, is not true. Contrary to this, travel ball is rarely available for Latin players. Instead, these players played baseball more naturally as children than in the US, where youth baseball is structured and organized. "One look at Latin countries will tell you that they still play and practice the way you and I did as kids," said Joe Barth. "Do you see any decline in their playing ability?" Among these organically grown players are Juan Soto, Miguel Cabrera, Vladimir Guerrero Jr, Rafael Devers, and Ronald Acuña Jr. Undeniably, they are as successful if not more so than those who have made their way through travel teams. There has been a steady climb of Latino players within the Majors Leagues since 2000. Demographic information collected during the 2022 season shows an increase in Latino players. Latino players now represent 28.5% of MLB rosters. Up from 16% just ten years ago. These demographics clearly show a trend that is of great concern within the College and Professional levels of the game.

So why does travel ball promote itself as *the way* to MLB or college baseball? It is very important for athletes and families to understand, not all travel baseball programs are created equal. The false narrative that many self-proclaimed elite travel programs promote is simply not accurate. While it is true that these travel programs did in fact have many prominent student-athletes wearing their uniforms, they were not always developed by these programs. In some cases, student-athletes that are promoted on various teams' websites only wore the uniform for a single game or tournament.

Many travel teams are simply a collection of talented athletes from various states that assemble each summer to wear a similar uniform. I know this because there are multiple organizations that still take credit for Tyler's success in baseball. Many travel programs have an actual recruiting coordinator who will cold call student-athletes from contact information available to subscribers on the Perfect Game site. They promise things such as better exposure, more national recognition, better opportunities to play at the NCAA D1 level, or even increased MLB draft opportunities. There is one common thread that many travel programs use to persuade families to play for their program, and it is one simple word: fear.

It is the mere fear of being left behind or missing out that is reinforcing in parents the need to invest thousands of dollars to get their children college exposure in some cases starting as early as eight years of age. The reality is that student-athletes all grow and mature at different ages and stages of life. Travel baseball is simply a platform that allows athletes the opportunity to gain increased exposure via a perceived higher level of competition. Travel teams are more than happy to show the rankings of their players who have been recruited but hide from communicating how many of them were not. More concerning is that these travel ball teams have not been as transparent with the student-athletes and their parents as most would think. In fact, most travel baseball participants are kept away from facts and truths. For the last ten or fifteen years, with the help of social media, these organizations have created incomes and lucrative careers that are essentially built on six to eight weeks during a summer. And what they've all been based on is a narrative that when you play on these teams, or within these programs, or you attend their showcases, your child will become a professional baseball player or a prominent college student-athlete. That narrative simply does not add up.

Travel baseball organizations also found parents were ready to pay a handsome sum of money if it meant getting their children into college baseball or possibly the draft. Parents began seeking out better travel programs regardless of the cost. They wanted to be a part of the better programs to wear their gear in hopes of catching a college coach's eye. It was as if they thought these travel uniforms were magic and would propel an athlete into the NCAA D1 landscape. In the beginning travel teams charged $1,000 per player. In an April 2010 article in Sports Illustrated, Guerry Baldwin quotes the cost of East Cobb Baseball at $1,400 per player. But after the 2013–2015 seasons, thanks to the power of social media–fueled marketing, some travel teams were charging anywhere from $2,500 to $8,000 per year! This was just to be on the team. On top of these team fees, parents were asked to pay for tournament gate fees, apparel and uniforms, lodging, travel, and food. Now it was not uncommon for parents of thirteen– through seventeen-year-olds to end up paying anywhere from $4000-$15,000 a year to play baseball.

I saw student-athletes being priced out of the game. Andrew McCutchen wrote about this in a February 2015 piece in *The Players Tribune* called "Left Out." "It's not about the $100 bat. It's about the $100-a-night motel room and the $30 gas money and the $300 tournament fee." Prior to travel ball, talent was restricted by geography. After the introduction of the travel ball, it was restricted by money. It's been argued that travel baseball lacks racial and socioeconomic diversity due to its high cost. This has caught the attention of both the NCAA and MLB. This issue must be addressed for baseball to become more accessible and inclusive. During the 1981 MLB season, the percentage of African American players peaked at 19%, in 2022 that number was slightly less than 8%. MLB is seeing tremendous growth in Latino and Asian players, while there is clearly a trend that shows that inner city neighborhoods as well as major metropolitan cities are no longer able to support local rec and little leagues. Is it due to a lack of interest in little league and rec baseball or is it the rise of the pay for play model that has taken over the youth baseball landscape? This topic is not solely the responsibility of major league baseball but also at the college level as well. While many college programs have made a concerted effort to maintain diversity awareness, most college baseball has also seen a lack of minority athletes during the recruiting process. During the 2022 season, at the NCAA D1 level, college rosters showed that less than 6% were African American. There is no need to point fingers but we as adults must begin to navigate the world of youth sports back into the focus of inclusion for all children and not just for those with financial means.

As travel ball grew, so did its offerings for younger players. I am not a proponent of travel baseball before the age of fourteen, or before high school. I have friends who own travel organizations, and their livelihood largely depends on the youth programs from the ages of six through thirteen. If you find that hard to believe, here's an example. Imagine a small travel ball organization. They offer a developmental program for ten-year-olds. Starting at age eleven, they have two teams per age group from 11U through 15U. Then they have showcase teams for 16U and 17U. Tuition averages around $3,000, and they have about thirteen players per team. (There would be fewer per team at the younger ages and more at the older ages due to pitcher-only players.) That "small" organization of thirteen teams and thirteen players per team makes $507,000 per year. Over half of that comes from players who are thirteen years old or younger. Every thirteen-player team that organization adds to its program is another $39,000 in revenue. Therefore, travel baseball organizations offer teams as young as 6U. It is not a player development model. It is a business development model.

Travel baseball over the last fifteen years has led to a massive decline in numbers at the rec ball levels. Once a staple of youth baseball, Little League suddenly saw a dramatic drop in signups. Parents were led to believe that their sons needed to be in a more competitive environment, or they would be less prepared for high school and even college baseball. In speaking with a father from Mississippi, I was told that at the 7U level a travel team said that the caliber of the travel team would make a difference on whether his son would be recruited for college baseball. Again, this was the father of a seven-year-old! These teams' owners are selling parents on nothing more than fear and greed. I want to state clearly that nothing your athlete does on a baseball field between the ages of six through thirteen is going to matter or mean *anything* to a college coach, not even a little bit! That is simply a massive sales pitch and one that you should simply say "no thank you" to.

As a parent, I want you to put yourself in the mind of your child as a six– to ten-year-old. This is the time of life for Santa Claus, Halloween, and the Easter Bunny. This is a time to believe in dreams of becoming anything and everything you want to be. It's about playing with friends, riding bikes, going fishing, and having ice cream after games. Now sit and listen to the travel ball games for those age groups. Listen to all the screaming and think about what your child is feeling in that moment. We are taking this magical time of childhood and making it about the grind. The current youth baseball landscape of lessons, travel baseball, tournaments, showcases, rings, and trophies weigh heavily on the minds of children. The pressure of not only living up to parental expectations but also classmates and friends. Children now live in a world of information overload. The lessons that they take sometimes are filled with words and theories that are difficult to understand let alone perform. We have suddenly shifted the focus of youth baseball from playing for enjoyment with peers and friends to parents now looking for metrics on 8-12 yr. old's regarding arm strength velocity and exit speed off bats. None of that really matters to a child unless parents or coaches make it an issue. This is a very heavy burden for a child to carry.

We have somehow become brainwashed into thinking a six-year-old will be hurt by an eight-year-old, or the eight-year-old will be hurt by a ten-year-old. "It's a problem," says Frank Niles. "It's not the whole problem, but there's way too many limitations put on kids … Adults have determined after decades of children of all ages playing with and against each other, that now kids might get hurt. It's a shame really. That's why as a high school coach what I must try to do is create a culture that any athlete can overcome what happens at practice or in a game." High school, college, American Legion, Babe Ruth—they're all played with a mix of ages. Basic athletic movements are learned through emulating our peers. Yet in youth travel baseball we go one year at a time. That is not a baseball development model. It is a business development model. It is done to create more revenue for the program. It has been proven in other sports such as basketball and soccer that children often rise to the challenge of competing with and against older student-athletes. It is not so much about the ages of athletes as much as it is about the ability levels. Children with advanced or above average skill sets will become bored and possibly regress if they are not mentally and physically challenged. A child learns everything in life from adults. They watch, listen, and learn. Why must youth sports be any different? A fifth-grade student-athlete can certainly play catch with a sixth or seventh grade athlete when no adults are present. Yes, a seventh grader may throw harder than a fifth grader but over a consistent period two things would happen. First the fifth grader would learn to catch a harder thrown ball as well as begin to throw harder themselves. This is true in most if not all aspects of life yet, no can do within youth baseball.

There's no such thing as a lesson to learn how to hit, or pitch, or field as a grade school–aged child, or there shouldn't be. At young ages a child simply needs to learn how to make contact with a baseball with their bat. We need to learn how to catch a baseball with a leather glove. We need to learn how to throw a baseball to a partner. That doesn't require money, but it does require time: with you as a parent, at the playground, or with friends. Joe Barth sees this emphasis on lessons impacting the quality of play as children get older. "I find it much more difficult to coach a high school player on how to run the bases. All the other decisions regarding baseball in his life are made by somebody else." Young athletes learn by watching and emulating and learning from their mistakes. Repetition will always lead to retention.

Contrary to the message of travel baseball teams, it is rec league baseball that will give children these repetitions. That is because many travel organizations have a win-at-all-costs environment. The elite players are given more playing time while the other players' progress is stunted. In rec leagues such as Little League or Cal Ripken Baseball, there are playing time requirements. This is important because children don't know what position they want to play at ages six through thirteen. They don't know if they're going to become a pitcher only or if they're going to be a switch hitter. Yet we have adults who have no business doing so telling children they can't switch hit or can't play shortstop or are only going to pitch. Even if your child is left-handed, let them play shortstop so they gain an understanding of what the position requires. Then they'll know, "That's a hard position to play." But how will they know that if they never had an opportunity to play it?

That brings me to another issue. Most travel programs are game heavy and practice light. That's a bad recipe for becoming a good student-athlete, learning what it takes to be a good teammate, and understanding what it takes to develop. However, the system is set up to be that way. Winning tournaments and rings or trophies lead to these programs becoming ranked, which in turn allows teams to use these rankings for promotion to future parents. The major issue with the number of games they play is the stress it puts on young players' bodies and more importantly their arms. In some cases, as many as three or four games could be played on a Saturday or Sunday. This format is a major issue that often leads to arm injuries.

Ask yourself this as an adult. Could you really play six baseball games in three days? Yet this is what we ask six– to thirteen-year-olds to do in travel baseball tournaments. Think of what that does to young arms. Think about the intensity and anxiety of playing tournaments every weekend. Games at the younger levels are supposed to be fun. Parents should seek a ratio of two to three practices per each game played. It is ok to seek out travel or rec programs that focus on development at younger ages. It is beneficial for parents to attend a few practices of a potential program for their child. Make sure that the instruction is consistent and taught with proper amount of practice repetitions. Make sure that athletes are seeing the field from all positions during practice setting thus ensuring that players are not stuck at one position. Young players develop much better in a repetition-based practice format. This allows young players to control the number of ground balls and fly balls that they field. It allows hitters to get consistent work on their swings. Strong practice habits that are learned early in an athlete's career will matter much more than playing meaningless games that are played hours away from home.

So many parents come to me saying their sons are losing their desire to play baseball at thirteen or fourteen. Now, some of that's natural. That's been going on for decades simply because there are alternatives, especially in today's world. But when you have student-athletes say it's not *fun* anymore, that's different. Think about why that's the case. Think about why it's so intense. It's because it's a business.

It is heart-wrenching to see how these young athletes and their families go through this. Time after time I have seen families become overwhelmed. They start to panic and wonder if they are not doing enough for their child. They begin to seek out the higher ranked program in hopes of gaining a spot on a more prominent travel team. The thought is, the bigger the program the greater the exposure, and therefore the greater the chances of the player being noticed by college coaches and MLB scouts. The fact is, no travel team is opening a door for a student-athlete. That young man is opening his own door. Travel teams are also not being forthright about the numbers. So, let's look at them.

There are 3.67 million children who play baseball between six and twelve years of age according to the Aspen Institute's State of Play 2022 report. Roughly 500,000 student-athletes play high school baseball. That's according to the NCAA's 2022–23 Guide for the College-Bound Student-Athlete. Perfect Game's own numbers reflect this decrease in opportunities as the competition level of the sport increases. There are 536 Perfect Game "Core" Tournaments scheduled for the 11U age group in 2023. These are tournaments run by full-time Perfect Game employees, with their scorekeepers scoring the games and their scouts recording velocities. At the 15U age group, there are 146 Perfect Game Core Tournaments scheduled. Three-hundred-ninety fewer, seventy-three percent drop—however you put it, it's a lot less.

What happens at the next level? That same NCAA guide shows that about 36,000 student-athletes play NCAA baseball (Divisions 1–3). Across all levels of college sports, which includes NAIA and JUCO (junior college), there are about 60,000 student-athletes playing baseball. Those aren't first-year students. That's across *all years of college*. Now let's look at the MLB draft. In 2022, there were 616 players selected out of college and high school.

As a parent, I understand the balancing act that we must provide for our children. On the one hand we want them to not only have and work towards their goals and dreams, but we also want them to understand the reality of how difficult it is to play the sport of baseball beyond high school. I vividly remember the night that Tyler, at the time sixteen years old, walked into my bedroom, looked me right in eye, and asked, "Do you think I'm really good enough to play at a school like Vanderbilt?" I turned the question around and said to him "The question needs to be, do you feel that you are good enough? It's easy for me as a dad to tell you that you are good enough, but you need to believe that you can play at that level. The reality will always be based on your work ethic and your own ability to believe in yourself when others around you may not."

There is no secret path and no script. Absolutely no one can promise your son a destination. The numbers show how truly incredibly difficult it is to play at the NCAA D1 level. In fact, it is only two percent of all high school players that ever reach that level. To play professionally is a minor and to become a major league player if only for a day is truly a miracle. There have been countless numbers of elite baseball athletes that simply were in the wrong organization at the wrong time. Imagine being a shortstop in the New York Yankees minor league system from 1995-2014. Unless you were traded, there was no path or room for you as a shortstop. If we were able to take every man that has ever played at the MLB level in the history of the game and put them all in Fenway Park, we would still have approximately 13,000 empty seats. Let that sink in for a minute.

Our children have dreams. Some dreams are more attainable than others, but their dreams need to be accepted, nurtured, and most importantly protected from those that offer false promises for their own financial gain. Surround your child with life mentors who offer your child a true understanding of what it will take to achieve their dreams and goals. These should be people who have made sacrifices, made tough decisions, and are examples for your child to see and listen to. As they get older, it is important we allow them to feel the pain of failure, so they understand the challenge that is ahead of them. We must allow them to understand the path ahead is filled with obstacles and hurdles that only they can get past.

However, the world of travel baseball wants you as a family to believe that because others who played for them achieved their goals, the travel organization has the answers and the plan. That is utter B.S. The answers that you and your son seek can only be answered within. Every single young athlete, regardless of the sport, learns and grows at a different speed. The most important factor to their success is accepting that no matter how many times life and the game of baseball knocks them down, they must continue to get back up and move forward.

The road to becoming a college-caliber baseball player and beyond is littered with could've, would've, and should've been. Your son must take ownership of his dream and turn a deaf ear to the naysayers and a blind eye to those that do not have his best interest in mind. There is no grind for young players. We often read on social media that young athletes must "grind" to play at higher levels. It is important that a young athlete has a foundation of love for the sport, young athletes should have fun and play rather than worry about high school or college at the young ages of 6-12. As a parent we must remember that he is always a little boy with a dream. When he falls, let him get himself back up. When he fails, never ask him why; ask him what he learned.

THE NUMBERS GAME

The numbers game is what also drives FOMO. After Tyler and Kyle graduated from college, I found myself answering questions and helping families regarding the college recruiting process. While I had been helping families since the late 1980s, the world of college recruiting was undergoing massive changes. The Prep Baseball Report, which started operations in 2005 as a subscription-based service, was now conducting showcases run by state directors. PBR began to challenge the Perfect Game ranking and showcase business. Many families were torn as to where to place their allegiance. Both Perfect Game and PBR promised rankings and regional and national showcases with hundreds of coaches in attendance. Many families started to double up by participating in multiple showcase events with both entities so that their athletes would not be slighted by the state, regional, and national rankings. Rankings sold subscriptions because every parent wanted to read the written reports on their student-athlete. A Perfect Game or PBR showcase revenue model might look something like this: state showcase $400, regional showcase $350, and the national showcase $250. Use those numbers to add up what a family might pay in addition to their travel team and travel fees. Every single PG and PBR regional and national event made for great content on many social media platforms. Those that had a highlight reel would post it on their Twitter and TikTok and hashtag college coaches across the country.

In a hashtag crazed world within social media, suddenly #uncommitted was attached to student-athletes as young as thirteen. Parents made it a point to put videos of their athletes online for the world to see. In the past, I would begin working with student-athletes and their families after the completion of their sophomore year. In the new world of travel baseball, families were now seeking guidance for college recruiting as young as eighth grade! They were now routinely seeing players at those younger ages committing to college programs, and parents felt as if college recruiting had now become a game of musical chairs. Parents began reaching out to me at a fever pitch wanting to see if their son was missing out, or what needed to be done to help get their son in front of college coaches.

Some, not all, parents would reach out and say something like, "My son is better than the young man that just committed to that school," or "How can a student-athlete that has yet to play a high school varsity game commit to that college?" It became common place for me to receive a text or email asking for my thoughts on various showcases or similar events for student-athletes in their freshman year or younger. One case was with a young man from New Hampshire. While talking with the student-athlete and family, I stressed how most college coaches wanted athletes to slow the process down. College coaches like late bloomers. They like those guys who are working to get better these first few years in high school, hitting the weight room, developing a little chip on their shoulder, and then in junior or senior year it comes together.

Rice University head coach Paul Janish spoke about this with me. "Super young recruiting is a game that is more marketing than it is anything else. And if you really keep track of guys who commit when they're in eight or ninth grade—if somebody did a study and really paid attention to where those kids end up, it's probably borderline comical." The other effect of travel ball he's seen is on players' stick-to-it-iveness. "There's not a whole lot of 'Hey, if you don't like it, play better.'" There's a "narrative, whether it be from home or in the car on the way home" that if you want to play a preferred position or if you want a better opportunity, you leave for it instead of working for it.

One family that I worked with beginning in 2016 was from Destrehan, Louisiana. The young man's name was Landon Marceaux. While living in Louisiana from 2011–2016 I met many families that I had helped: Daniel Cabrera (LSU) from River Ridge, Jack Burk (U of Lafayette) from New Orleans, Mason Koppens (Northeastern University) from Metairie, Kaleb Roper (Tulane University) from Kenner, and Connor Poche (Centenary College of Louisiana) from Lutcher. I had established the ability to help student-athletes and families, and Joey Marceaux, Landon's dad, asked me to look at his son as a pitcher.

Now at the time Landon had just wrapped up his eighth-grade year and come to my facility in Jefferson, LA. Landon was approximately five foot eight and under 150 pounds. As I watched Landon warm up, it was immediately apparent that this young man took baseball very seriously. He had a great warm up routine and every detail was his own, meaning he didn't need me or his father to tell him how to stretch or prepare to warmup. Once Landon was loose, I had him get up on the mound and begin to throw. One key detail when evaluating young pitchers is to watch how the three levers work. The three levers being, in order, the elbow, wrist and fingers. When a college coach is watching high school age pitchers, this is a key area that they focus on. All young throwers should lead with their elbows if possible.

As I watched the first few pitches coming out of Landon's hand it was easy to see that he had the gift of pitching. He was smaller in size but already displayed a strong feel for the craft of pitching. One thing that I pride myself on is the ability to recognize talent and ability at younger ages. Daniel Cabrera was twelve when I first saw him hit. Daniel ended up becoming a second-round draft selection of the Detroit Tigers in 2020. Another young man from Gulfport, Mississippi, was Brendan Hardy. Now Brendan was a shortstop on the same team as Landon. They played youth baseball together on a team called the Crescent City Hooks. Brendan's dad Bill was a minor leaguer with the Detroit Tigers in the 1990s and wanted Brendan to be a shortstop in the worst way, largely because Brendan had a very strong arm. One day at a practice inside my facility I asked Brendan if he wanted to try pitching. After some initial reluctance by his dad, Brendan got up on the mound. Instantly I could see that his future was most definitely going to be on the hill. His father Bill laughed at the thought and kidded with me about a crystal ball. Well, in June of 2018 the New York Mets drafted Brendan as a pitcher.

So, as I was watching Landon pitch, I took some video and sent it off to a few college coaches, one of which was Tim Corbin at Vanderbilt. Within a few minutes Tim shot back a quick response, "Boy does his arm work well. He uses all three levers really well." Now it is important to understand that the video was not meant for recruiting purposes; it was simply a way to provide feedback to Landon and his dad. I recommended to both that I felt it would benefit Landon to attend a few events during the summer with the Evoshield Canes National program.

In Louisiana travel baseball was not a big deal as high school coaches were also American Legion coaches. Many high school coaches frowned upon travel baseball, instead preferring that their athletes stay local. After much discussion Landon and his father agreed to take part in the summer travel schedule. Landon was, by travel baseball terminology, a rising freshman. Now remember, in 2015 travel baseball was at its pinnacle, and when Landon took the mound in Fort Meyers, Florida, he was a complete unknown. Small-framed by right-handed pitcher standards, he was not physically imposing but he sure knew how to pitch. I had to convince the Canes coaching staff not to let his size fool them. Then right on cue, Landon proceeded to throw four shutout innings against a very talented Orlando Scorpions 15U team. It was on this day that schools such as UVA, UNC, and LSU could not believe what they were seeing. Landon displayed impeccable command with three above average pitches. He even caught the eyes of Team USA coaching staff. Landon went on to play for the 18U Team USA National team and Louisiana State University. He was selected in the second round of the 2021 MLB draft.

All the athletes mentioned above benefited greatly from the contacts that I had within the college coaching community as well as participating with great national travel baseball organizations such as GBG, owned by Michael Garciaparra (Nomar's brother), and the Evoshield Canes, owned by Jeff Petty. The early to mid-2010s were what I would term its peak. For the ten years prior, travel baseball was truly and undeniably the place to be each summer as far as college recruiting was concerned. It started to change in 2014, with the opening of the massive LakePoint Sports Complex in Cartersville, GA, where Perfect Game had signed a twenty-year lease. Travel baseball suddenly became more accessible for many travel programs that had spent the previous years on the outside looking in.

Teams with a rich history began to franchise or outright buy regional or local travel programs. Seemingly overnight, the travel baseball world was filled with Southeast, West Coast, Mid Atlantic, and Northeast versions of these different organizations. The thought was that by not only changing the name of a team but by wearing the nationally known team's logo and gear, roster sizes would get a boost. The other part of the sales pitch was that franchised and purchased teams would get access to many of the bigger events across the country. Remember the teams I mentioned in The Early Years of Travel Ball? Here is how some of them had grown by 2017.

- Banditos: sixty-six teams in four states
- Canes: forty-six teams in six states
- Dirtbags: fourteen teams in two states
- East Cobb Baseball: fifty-one teams in two states
- Scorpions: twenty-six teams in two states

While on the surface it may seem that this was a benefit, it soon became clear that many of these teams were not the same caliber as the parent, national teams. The people who did benefit were the owners who were generating life-changing income.

Young, entrepreneurial former college and pro players (or coaches) saw the business of travel baseball as a career endeavor, and a lucrative one at that. Suddenly there was an abundance of travel teams in every state. Facilities and teams began to multiply by the hundreds. No longer was there a need for families to travel hours to play on a team. Lessons, instruction and recruiting services were in every major city and town across the country. A travel team simply needed to hang a sign that touted their involvement with either Perfect Game or Prep Baseball Report.

Showcases were sprouting up across the country, too. Indoor showcases in the colder climates and outdoor showcases in the west and south. Tournaments were held from January through November. Over the past five to six years, these previously meaningful and ultra-competitive events have now become grossly watered down and meaningless. Now families are routinely sent emails and invitations to attend over-hyped championships. Perfect Game, PBR, Future Series, and even NTIS Team USA are all vying for families' money. Each of these entities promote rankings and championships; they are business-driven events, not baseball development events. Families now play in all sorts of age-based world series and regional and national tournaments, often multiple times each year. There are wood bat national events, aluminum bat national events, and even financially driven All-American events. In the early years, Perfect Game created these events for the country's elite athletes to compete against each other. No amount of money would have guaranteed entry into any of those early championships. Now that has given way to an open pay-for-play opportunity. Anyone with the funds can gain entry.

You really can't understand how much travel ball has grown from its small beginnings until you look at the numbers. Luckily, Perfect Game lets you search for tournaments all the way back to 1995 on their website. In 2002 they held one tournament in July, the WWBA 18U National Championship. In 2003 they added a tournament and called them Junior Division and Senior Division WWBA national championships. In 2005 they broke it into four different tournaments for 15U, 16U, 17U, and 18U. It stayed that way until 2012, when they added a 14U wood bat tournament and a 12U metal bat tournament. Seven-hundred-twenty-three teams played in East Cobb that month. In 2014 it grew to seven tournaments, which were now being held at LakePoint. Attendance was up to 849 teams across five age divisions. In 2015 that exploded to twenty-one tournaments, ten age divisions from 9U to 18U, and 1,357 teams. This was all in one month in one state. In 2022 there were eight tournaments, six age divisions from 13U through 18U, and 1,612 teams. To put this in perspective, the 2010 WWBA National Championship that Tyler competed in had 210 teams. That same tournament in 2022 had 434 teams competing. Nationwide, only nine Perfect Game tournaments were held in July of 2010. In July of 2022 that number was 381.

What drove college coaches and scouts to these events in the previous years was the competitiveness of each program and the athletes on all the rosters. In those early years, you had to have an above average ability level to not only make a travel team but, more importantly, to play in these events. Every game, whether it was pool play or championship rounds, mattered to coaches and scouts. College coaches are now seeing a very watered-down caliber of play at the pool play levels. Scores have become lopsided, and often top tier teams are spread out to ensure they face each other during the championship rounds. The college coaches and scouts who once flocked to these events from beginning to end are now routinely waiting for the playoff rounds to begin digging into the evaluations.

It is clear that greed, not an increase in the quantity of quality players, was truly driving the growth of the travel baseball landscape.

I interviewed University of Delaware head coach Greg Mamula, who said, "As the number of teams in tournaments has expanded over the years, the overall talent level within each tournament has certainly decreased … The days of just showing up to a complex without a planned schedule are gone. Organization and scheduling are king at these tournaments." John McCormack, head coach at Florida Atlantic University, shares that perspective. "They are not as strong as they used to be because there are so many teams now." Mike Baxter, recruiting coordinator at Vanderbilt University, says they focus more on their own camps and recommendations from people in their network. He said camps are an opportunity to "coach the kids" and see how they respond. Vanderbilt is trying to find out things they can't learn from a tournament or showcase. "What's the aptitude like? What's the personality like? Does he like the way that we go with our [coaching staff's] personal kind of energy and styles … It's a very key piece in our process and a lot of our players have come through our camp."

Families need to understand that now more than ever, college coaches and MLB scouts are not concerned with what team an athlete plays for. In recent conversations with many college coaches, they all utter similar things: student-athletes today feel that they are customers, players think they deserve an opportunity because it has been paid for, and at the college level it's about physicality and performance. That is a key message: if you have the necessary strength and you perform, you can play. I always try to inform families that the number one area to focus their time and resources on at the ages of thirteen through eighteen is physicality. Strength, speed, and size. A student-athlete's physicality is a student-athlete's personal billboard. A coach can see that a student-athlete has discipline and a routine by looking at his body.

So why would Perfect Game water down travel baseball? This is only my opinion, but I think the answer is money. The 2022 17U WWBA National Championship had a $3,150 entry fee. That's $1,367,100 in entry fees from one tournament. Then there are the gate fees. Every tournament is different, but this one offered a $65 pass to all games or $12 daily passes. Frank Niles joked that back in the day if the Seadogs lost during pool play, he would tell people, "Hey we finished first because we've lost two games and we're heading home." Nowadays, tournaments have consolation games. It's all about revenue for event holders: gate fees, concession stands, and merchandise. They also must justify the team entry fees for these tournaments.

As an aside, nationally known travel programs continue to thrive. Here's how many teams these programs have registered with Perfect Game for the 2023 season.

- Banditos: fifty-five teams in Texas
- Canes: sixty teams in five states
- Dirtbags: forty-three teams in five states
- East Cobb Baseball: sixty-five teams in three states
- Scorpions: twenty-seven teams in four states

Youth baseball has become a big business. No one foresaw the entire industry of youth sports would become the darling of the businesspeople and venture capital investors. But perhaps we should have.

THE BU$INE$$ OF YOUTH BASEBALL

I've said the sport of youth baseball is big business. How big is big? The *State of Play 2022* report by Project Play helps us understand. We've already learned that 3.67 million six– to twelve-year-olds are playing baseball. Another 1.98 million thirteen– to seventeen-year-olds play. That includes children playing travel or rec league who may not make their high school team. Project Play found that families spend $714 per season on average for their child to play baseball. That's everyone from the four-year-old t-ball player to the seventeen-year-old attending showcases. That makes youth baseball at least a $4-billion industry, and it's growing. Their data show overall participation in travel sports has more than doubled from spring of 2021 to fall of 2022. Wintergreen Research predicts the overall youth sports market will triple from 2019 to 2026. That would put baseball at $10–12 billion per year. I'll say it again. Baseball is big business.

It's so big that it impacts the communities where tournaments are held. A June 6, 2014, article in the *Rome News-Tribune* reported the economic impact of a single, sixty-five team tournament held at LakePoint to be $1 million. Prospect Meadows in Iowa is another Perfect Game tournament host. Their website states that in 2021 they brought 40,000 people to Marion, IA, and the surrounding area. Event attendees spent $10 million that year.

Now, tournaments are vital for all travel programs, as they justify each program's team fee. Why should a family pay thousands a year in tuition if their son isn't going to a brand name showcase or tournament? Some organizations such as East Cobb, Canes, Five Star, and Dirtbags conduct their own tournaments on an annual basis with many major college programs agreeing to attend. What families don't know is often the tournament directors/owners receive kickbacks from the local hotels and restaurants, which can be extremely lucrative. Many see a return of ten to as much as twenty percent on hotel bookings and meals eaten. That's on top of entry fees, gate fees, concessions, and merchandise sales. Understanding this, it's easy to understand what started happening next.

In 2022, Rick Thurman and Rob Ponger bought Perfect Game. Thurman is a former MLB agent who founded the agency Beverly Hills Sports Council. Ponger is a former IMG executive. IMG is known for representing athletes in endorsement deals, producing, and distributing media content, and for its IMG Academy in Florida, a private school focused on developing elite athletes. This is a major shift for the travel baseball world. Now it may seem as not a big deal for parents as most never knew or met Perfect Game founder Jerry Ford. This is a shift from a baseball person—who had the original intention of bringing coaches, scouts, and the most talented players together—to businesspeople.

Recently, Perfect Game started taking over USSSA (United States Specialty Sports Association) tournaments. USSSA is another youth tournament organization that is so large they have their own bat certification. There is a very good reason why the new ownership wanted to expand their number of youth tournaments. Allow me to take you under the microscope of youth travel baseball. Over the last two years in the post-COVID era, families were hungry for a return to normal. Family and athletic events that had to shut down for most of 2020 and part of 2021 began to reappear. Perfect Game capitalized on this by holding events all year long for age groups such as 9U–13U.

What do you as a parent feel is the real reason for these events? If you guessed entry fees and gate fees, you are only scratching the surface. These events have little to no barriers to entry. That means they are usually well attended by athletes and their families from across the country. To compete in these events, parents are asked to fill out player profiles. Now as a parent you may think this is a simple request. You are providing data to Perfect Game that they can use in a myriad of ways over the upcoming years ahead. An MLB insider explained it to me like this. "Perfect Game is trying to get the younger market because the older market they lost from a quality standpoint. They're trying to indoctrinate you at younger ages." Information such as birthdays, graduation year, email addresses, cell phone, and mailing addresses are all entered Perfect Game's systems. It is then used to try to turn you into a paying customer for your child's entire athletic career. PG also sells any or all a family's information. Ever wonder how all this college email and snail mail finds its way to you? The mere fact that you as a family are willing to travel nationally for a child as young as nine years old tells college camps, independent showcases, and equipment companies that you are willing to spend money on your athlete.

Now, you may also be thinking that by attending these events, you will help your athlete regarding individual state and national rankings. Players are given scouting reports and rankings by Perfect Game employees. On Twitter, Perfect Game Youth posts clips and talks about the hand speed, barrel control, and two-strike approach of middle school students. A ranking at nine to thirteen years old, while extremely important to your athlete, means little to the decision-makers in the game. Upon closer inspection, the rankings are about creating additional revenue. Parents are asked to subscribe monthly so that they can read blogs about events their son attended and to see if he is ranked according to Perfect Game. Youth teams can now boast about the number of ranked players on their teams, which of course is all a marketing plan. Teams can also brag about where they are ranked as a program both regionally as well as nationally. It is a repeat of what happened at the high school–aged levels of the sport in the 2010s.

There are other ways Perfect Game makes money off parents. They partnered with Skill Show to produce all the videos for their events. Do you want a video of your son at a showcase or tournament? Pay Skill Show. They developed their own game scoring app called DiamondKast as a direct competitor to the GameChanger app. However, GameChanger is still used at some tournaments, leaving parents with two apps to purchase if they want access to all stats. If we simply follow all the money that is created at the youth levels of baseball, it is easy to understand why many families struggle financially to afford this type of travel over a period of eight to ten years.

We talked earlier about how even a relatively small, local program can generate several hundred thousand dollars in revenue per year. Many—if not most—of these travel baseball programs were owned by former student-athletes who had started their programs in their early twenties with not much of a business management background. They were great baseball people but not always experienced businesspeople. There was a lack of understanding of things like margins and break-even points. As is often the case when large sums of monies are generated, venture capitalists began to take a deeper look into the business of baseball. These investors saw that the revenue would be perennial. For every family exiting the travel baseball process at seventeen, a new family at ten (or nine, eight, seven, or even six) years of age would be entering. They also saw the inexperience of existing owners and made a common sales pitch: sell the travel baseball organization, stay on as a coach, and let the businesspeople run the business.

USA Prime is an example of a program that grew this way. It started in 2017 with an investment from JF2 Capital. They now have sixty-seven teams registered for 2023 with Perfect Game, play in nine divisions from 9U to 18U, and have locations in 11 states. Their website says the "are the largest full service amateur baseball organization in the United States." There have been pictures posted on Instagram of their 15U players ready to board a private plane. This is what college coaches mean when they say high school student-athletes are being catered to.

3Step Sports LLC is another venture capital–backed company with a growing presence in youth baseball. Its founder, David Geaslen was the founder and CEO of Scouts, Inc. in the early 2000s. After its purchase by ESPN, he was ESPN's vice president of high school sports and recruiting. He then founded and led a youth and high school sports media company, NE Sports. In 2016 he started 3STEP Sports. The company oversees club teams, national events, content creation, custom apparel, team travel, and facility management.

They are a one-stop youth sports solution. 3STEP is club operator, event operator, club owner, or league owner in baseball, basketball, combat sports, fastpitch, field hockey, football, lacrosse, soccer, and volleyball. They produce and sell media content used by major outlets such as Baseball America, ESPN, Gatorade Player of the Year, the NFL Draft, and USA Today. They own fourteen sports facilities in Maine, Massachusetts, New Hampshire, and Pennsylvania, and partner with facilities Indiana, Maine, Massachusetts, and Texas. Their business also includes travel services and apparel. According to a report in Sports Business Journal, 3STEP Sports had 30 employees in 2018. In 2019 they got an outside investment from Juggernaut Capital and Fiume Capital. As of 2022, 3STEP is a $250-million business with 700 employees.

In 2017, Geaslen also became part of the Baseball Americas ownership team and was its president for a period of time. That same year, Baseball America partnered with Perfect Game to grow the youth game (14U and younger) through coverage in its website and magazine and by co-branding some events. However, the youth game is no longer covered on Baseball America's website, and they have a new president as of 2021.

One of the biggest services of 3STEP is its content management within high school sports. They partner with ESPN 100 (boys' basketball), ESPN HoopGurlz (girls' basketball), and ESPN 300 (football) recruiting databases. They cover baseball via Baseball America and provide high school sports coverage for USA Today. The social media marketing and content management are all skillfully executed; they're part of the way student-athletes are used to create revenue. Successful student-athletes and their achievements are promoted and used to entice parents into allow their children to participate in these highly promoted events. The marketing of these athletes create a true fear that if other student-athletes do not attend these promoted events, then they will be left behind.

In contrast to USA Prime, 3STEP does not change the names of the companies it acquires. The Bay Sox, Nor'Easters, Show New England, New Hampshire Prospects, Seacoast Pirates, Grizzlies Baseball Club, and NH Cannons are all part of 3STEP. The upside of venture capitalists taking over youth travel baseball was that suddenly these programs were being run like business, with an eye on profit margins as opposed to talent levels. The more the merrier. No room on this year's 16U team? No problem! Simply create another team, thus adding to the bottom line. One of the programs owned by 3STEP fields *five* 16U teams.

In an interview with Inside Lacrosse, Geaslen spoke about the company having more resources than others in the youth sports industry. "But really what we have is everybody pulling in the same direction ... We're one. Our financials, our employees, everyone rolls up into one." It is no big deal for 3STEP Sports to buy a successfully running business and add it to its umbrella.

Perfect Game does not have as large of a presence in New England as it does elsewhere. What does have a presence is the Select League, owned by 3STEP. It offers travel league play from April through mid-June for the youth players, and from mid-June through July for the high school age divisions. There is the Select Experience, showcase-style events where 10U to 14U players are filmed and graded. Select Events are tournaments held at facilities owned by 3STEP.

Think about how this works for a family. They pay tuition to a travel program, purchase their son's required team apparel (and maybe a hoodie or team polo shirt for themselves), book a hotel through a travel service, pay gate fees at a tournament facility, and buy a t-shirt for their son to remember the tournament by. Unless they are paying attention, they don't understand that the money from all those purchases is going to the same parent company. Then the company takes all the revenue that comes in each year and continues to buy more organizations, fields, tournaments, and apparel companies. It looks like 3STEP Sports is on a journey of establishing a monopoly in the youth sports industry.

The shift is that a team owner is no longer merely a former college or pro athlete. One must wonder, are the best interests of student-athletes and their families now all about a corporate bottom line? Are profit margins more important than youth development? I agree that we live in a capitalist society. The key point is that many families are not truly aware of the net being cast over the entire youth baseball world. I simply want parents to be informed about what is driving the continued growth of pay-for-play youth baseball. Over the last five years I feel the venture capital investors have begun to put youth sports on the same level as pork bellies, citrus, and oil, treating them as a commodity. Their roots have penetrated everywhere. I worry that soon they will own all revenue streams within youth sports. They will make money from every dollar spent within travel, lodging, the apparel company, the baseball equipment, coaches, supplements, vitamins, and nutrition.

The truth is that no matter how much businessmen try to proclaim that they are working for the betterment of baseball or trying to ease stress for the players, they are utterly fooling the players and the parents. The game of baseball is no longer a game of skill sets and talent. It is a game of resources and means that is played through deception and fear. In that same Inside Lacrosse interview, Geaslen was asked about whether the stability of the youth sports market influenced venture capital firms' decision to invest in 3STEP. He confirmed it was and described the industry as "recession proof" because of parents' desire to support their children's interests.

The mere fact that no family wants to miss out is enough to keep adding to the $4-billion industry of youth baseball. Parents need to become better informed and educated. Understand that the money being spent to play youth sports should be no different than the money spent on a family vacation. It is purely about moments, memories, and relationships. High school and college opportunities are not determined by any amount of money; it will always be about skill sets and talent.

The transition that takes place after a student-athlete's high school career ends is critical to understand. During the travel baseball years, many parents often look for customer service or a return on their investment. If they did not like how their son was treated or there were limited playing opportunities, they simply moved on to a new program. This travel ball mindset has led to the NCAA changing the rules for the transfer portal, which I'll cover more later. However, unlike the business of travel baseball, college coaches are unaffected by the thoughts or opinions of parents. When Tyler attended Vanderbilt, there were many times when I had to bite my tongue and allow him to handle his own business. It is important for parents to understand that your son must understand his opportunities to get between the lines are earned. Nothing he has done in the past matters to a college program. To quote *The Godfather*, "Nothing personal, it's just business." If a student-athlete is not physically and mentally prepared to compete at their full capacity in the fall, they will be left behind and left with limited options.

CHANGES AT THE TOP

In just the past two years, we saw some incredible changes in the NCAA. Many of these changes are likely to fill in the vacuum left by the realignment of the MLB's minor league system, where 160 teams were reduced to just 120. In this chapter, I will be discussing the main changes that have been introduced in the NCAA over the past few years, and how the NCAA is expected to evolve alongside these new implementations.

Roster Size Changes

Due to the changes brought about by the provision of an extra year of eligibility, the NCAA is now allowing schools to have roster sizes of between 35 to 40. However, athletes beyond 35 will have to be a player that was previously affected by the loss of a season due to COVID. Teams will be allowed to have between 27 to 32 players on scholarship, but athletes in the 28-32 range will have to be part of the group of athletes who lost a season to COVID.

Under NCAA's original rules, a D1 baseball team's 11.7 scholarships may be divided between a maximum of 27 players, with all students having to receive a minimum of 25 percent of a scholarship. It is important to note the players on the extra roster spots would also count against this rule.

The roster size rule changes were ostensibly made to accommodate the returning seniors, and it is highly likely that we will be seeing many returning seniors for the next couple of seasons. This is because a strong majority of coaches are leaning towards asking seniors to return for an extra year of eligibility. This is also an expected move, and these seniors are likely to be the most experienced and skilled players on the field. These senior players want to stay and exhaust every opportunity they may have to play professionally and improve their draft chances. This is a win–win scenario for college programs and MLB teams because they now have older college lineups that are more competitive and talented.

The fact that college rosters are now filled with older, mature athletes adds an additional layer of difficulty for incoming freshman athletes. It is now imperative for them to be prepared from both a strength and skill set perspective before they step foot on campus. They must get their mind and body prepared for the extremely difficult fall that is ahead of them. Fall rosters at the college level can be extremely challenging. As many as sixty athletes are competing for a thirty-five-man roster spot. The bottom line is that fall season at the college level is make-or-break time. Often times there are highly talented freshmen who simply find out they are not ready for the level of play. They are told at the end of the fall in an exit meeting that they will not be added to the spring roster. This is a cold and harsh reality and many are simply cut or told to transfer.

This is why many families are now researching the value and importance of either junior college or a postgraduate year. If your student-athlete is strong academically, I strongly suggest taking a serious look at postgraduate opportunities. The postgraduate and junior college opportunities offer a student-athlete the ability to add the physical and mental maturation they may need to be completely prepared for the four-year college experience. The elimination of short-season minor league teams and twenty rounds of the draft have created an entirely new landscape at the college baseball level, as you'll read.

Elimination of 42 MILB Teams

As briefly mentioned above, many short season teams in minor league baseball were eliminated in December 2020, with a total of 42 minor league teams being removed from the original list of 162. The bottom-performing teams had very few fans who showed up at their games and were thus justifiably cut. In addition, MLB mentioned that one of the main reasons for these eliminations was that the facilities of these teams were not up to standard. However, the implications of this elimination are significant. I believe that there is a gradual shift that is occurring, where the MLB is slowly beginning to rely more on the NCAA as a developmental arm for future players.

While there are instances where there are going to be excellent players recruited right out of high school, these occurrences are extremely rare. Players generally develop at a much more rapid pace in college than in the minor leagues. This is largely attributed to college coaches being much more consistent and professional. Furthermore, these coaches generally put in longer hours and are much more detailed. Simply put, the players that are coming out of the NCAA have been developed to their fullest potential, and the MLB has recognized this.

For that reason, the MLB has likely found it difficult to rationalize spending money at the lower levels in the minor leagues where a vast majority of players will never make it the beyond double A. MLB teams could now recruit a graduating senior, get them to play for a summer, and then decide whether to retain the player or to simply recruit another senior, based on his performance. With more and more college students entering the MLB as compared to high school students becoming the trend, this will likely result in a larger number of future MLB players being trained and developed within the NCAA.

An Extra Year of Athletic Eligibility

On March 30, 2020, the NCAA voted to allow athletes whose seasons were cut short by COVID-19 to play for another year. However, there was a condition tied to this extra year. Athletes would not be offered a full scholarship for that extra and had to pay either some or all the cost of attendance. One of the most misunderstood aspects of college baseball is the scholarship allotment. Unlike most sports offered at the NCAA D1 level, baseball is only allowed 11.7 full scholarships that must be divided amongst 27 student-athletes. In 2023 the traditional maximum spring roster size of 35 returns. A full baseball scholarship is as rare as a unicorn at the college level. If an athlete is offered a full baseball scholarship it will typically be an elite, MLB-draft-caliber pitching prospect.

Also misunderstood is that baseball scholarships are one-year agreements. They are production based. If a student-athlete proves to be of significant value to a college program, then their scholarship is usually extended or increased the following year. If an athlete fails to live up to the projection or production, their scholarship can be reduced or even taken away. Exit meetings, which are one-on-one meetings between a head coach and student-athlete, are held twice a year, once at the completion of the fall season and again at the completion of the spring season. These meetings can be extremely challenging for both college coaches and the student-athletes.

With the completion of the 2023 season the extra years of eligibility will for most, expire. The lone exception will be for junior college athletes, who in some cases were given two extra years of eligibility. Through this move, athletes gained another chance at pursuing a four-year college opportunity and completing their college baseball career on a high note, which would provide them with a greater chance at being drafted. This provision of an extra year of athletic eligibility signaled the importance of the NCAA to the MLB. There has been a drastic increase in the proportion of MLB draft picks who are college athletes. The NCAA fulfilled their capacity by providing seniors with a chance to regain their "lost years" and widen the pool for the future MLB drafts. Seniors with five to six years of experience coming out of college baseball experience are in some cases extremely attractive to MLB teams, but not for the reason you may think. These older athletes have little to no leverage. These older players allow MLB teams to draft experienced athletes who are given a short window of opportunity within the MILB system. This trend is likely to continue in the future, exacerbated by the contraction of minor leagues.

One Time Transfer with Immediate Eligibility

On April 28, 2020, the NCAA instituted a change that would allow student-athletes to transfer once in their careers and have immediate eligibility to play for their new schools. Prior to this, students were penalized by being forced to sit out for the first season at their new school, which heavily discouraged transfers. This new rule has completely changed college baseball across the nation.

To begin, coaches are going to have to switch from approaching coaching as a long-term plan to a short-term one. Previously, coaches recruited players with the intent of developing them across their entire college baseball career. They may have prioritized innate talent, potential, and coachability over raw skill. However, this new transfer rule is going to change all of that.

Coaches now have another source of recruiting players to starting roles and will also have to start worrying about losing players via the same avenue. Schools are expected to shift part of their focus on recruiting to seeking out experienced college student-athletes from other schools that understand the college routine both academically as well as athletically. This is detrimental to high school recruits. A greater share of resources is going to be diverted towards attracting and retaining talent at the highest levels at the expense of new recruits.

It is important for families and student-athletes to truly understand one major point as a high school recruit: colleges are allowed to have expanded rosters during fall baseball. This means that walk-on student-athletes, student-athletes that may have transferred into a university later in the process, as well as returning athletes can often create fall rosters well in excess of sixty student-athletes that are competing for thirty-five spring roster spots. Fall baseball at the college level is a *highly* competitive environment. It is not uncommon for newly recruited athletes to be told that there is no room for them on the spring roster. While it does not seem fair or truthful, I can assure you that there have been many college freshman athletes that have been told that there will not be any roster spots available and that they should look to transfer to a JUCO program or another program. I often advise families to look at fall rosters across all levels of college baseball. It is appropriate to ask a college coach how big of a fall roster they carry and how that may affect your son. College athletics are about fielding competitive teams that can compete year in and year out.

College coaches are now going to shift towards assembling new teams year by year, depending on who they are able to obtain via the transfer portal and what current athletes they can retain. Talented players who are kept as backups and have the potential to develop may instead choose to leave and play a starting role elsewhere. The best teams in the country are going to become stronger with each year as they have the leverage to pick and choose students from other schools.

This also means that college athletes will be expected to be at the top of their game consistently, as they may find themselves being pushed aside to make way for new transfers if they do not perform up to expectations or perhaps are injured. Hence, if you want to make it in college baseball, you are going to have to be prepared to work extremely hard every year of your career. The days of athletes having the luxury of time across their whole career to develop are gone. The executive director of the American Football Coaches Association sums up the general sentiment across all college sports as "…it's not developing players anymore…it's about assimilating a team for next year that can win."

Multiple Transfer Windows

In August of 2022, The NCAA D1 baseball committee voted to make changes that would allow baseball student-athletes who want to transfer to now have multiple transfer windows during a season. This rule went into effect as of Sept 1, 2022

Previously, baseball athletes could enter the portal by notifying the coaching staff and filling out proper paperwork to enter the portal by a July 1 deadline. Now, the NCAA has added a pair of transfer windows. This change was brought about as the NCAA wanted to allow student-athletes the flexibility to react to family or academic issues. An example of this might be a student-athlete that had a parent get sick or become ill and required a student-athlete to be closer to home. It allows athletes and their families to not feel that they have limited options. Many times, after the completion of a fall season a student-athlete realizes that his opportunities will be limited in the spring. This new rule now allows a student-athlete at the NCAA D1 level to explore possible JUCO opportunities if they are freshmen or sophomores. An upperclassman could be seeking playing time at lower levels of NCAA or NAIA.

The NCAA directors approved a window that is 45 days from the day postseason selections are made in baseball. This allows student-athletes the appropriate amount of time to see the course the baseball was taking, coaching staff changes, roster turnover etc. The deadline for a student-athlete to enter transfer paperwork in 2023 will be July 13 for the first window. There are several reasons for the mid-July transfer window. Some student-athletes begin to determine whether the MLB will become a reality as well as college programs that feel they are over exposed to the MLB draft will begin to aggressively seek to fill these roster voids with seasoned athletes that will be playing in various summer collegiate programs. Another twist to the July 13th date as opposed to July 1, is that often college summer teams are comprised of athletes from college programs from all over the country. Suddenly a student-athlete from a smaller or lower-level program begins to demonstrate advanced ability, and a summer teammate will convince that athlete to transfer into a bigger perceivably better program.

One of the ramifications of MLB pushing their amateur draft from early June to mid-July has now caused college coaches to have many sleepless nights. These coaches must now wait an extra month before having roster certainty. They must now identify possible areas of needs if they lose current athletes from their rosters as well as potential incoming high school recruits. They need to be able to evaluate potential transfers from other programs. This is an area that greatly affects high school student-athletes. This past fall, many high school athletes who had signed letters of commitment were told at the last minute—and in some cases while already enrolled in their summer classes—that there not be any opportunities for them.

The second period for spring student-athletes will be December 1–15. An important clarifier for this time as it pertains to baseball is that it changes nothing about the prohibition on mid-year transfers. Unlike softball, baseball players entering the portal during this period still must sit out until the next baseball season and would not be permitted to play during the upcoming season. So as an example, this fall several LSU athletes were told that they would not have spring roster spots. If they wanted to laterally transfer during the second transfer period, they would have to sit out the upcoming spring season and then become part of an active roster in the fall.

There are important exceptions to the above. An athlete is granted a lateral transfer opportunity if there are changes to staff or the head coach after the completion of the fall season, or if athletic aid is reduced, canceled, or not renewed.

Suspension of Prior Name, Image, and Likeness Rules

Prior to June 30, 2021, the NCAA regarded athletes as amateurs, and thus disallowed them from receiving any form of endorsements. Any rule violations meant that athletes were no longer allowed to play. However, all of this changed after the Supreme Court ruled that the NCAA were unable to prevent colleges from making education-related payments to college athletes. Following that, the Name, Image, and Likeness (NIL) policy was suspended, and student-athletes are now going to be able to profit from their NIL.

The new opportunities that have opened are plentiful. For instance, brands such as Sam's Club and Dollar Shave Club have partnered with student-athletes to promote their own products or services, which has generated substantial income for these athletes.

Following this change, there has also been an uptick in social media activity amongst student-athletes, as we have seen many individuals who have cultivated large social media followings being able to benefit directly from this change as companies sought them out for sponsorship deals. Players will now be able to start building their brand from the start of their careers, and this provides them with an excellent opportunity to maximize the benefits that they will derive from their college baseball careers. In addition, the extra funding channeled into endorsement deals makes college sports much more attractive than before, and it is likely that competition for college baseball starting lineups will get more intense in the future. High profile incoming freshman baseball players may now view college baseball to increase their personal brand, and this can create animosity within a program. Many college coaches that used to have boosters that helped finance their sport are now facing reduced aide as that now is being used in some cases for NIL packages. It is important for families to understand that any NIL deal is going to be based on performance. Nothing in the world of college baseball is guaranteed, it is all based on performance.

However, there is another cause for concern from coaches that students with established social media followings may find themselves receiving numerous NIL deals, while their teammates may struggle to secure even a single NIL deal. This may require coaches to delicately balance the different sets of egos on their teams and ensure that students remain laser-focused on the game instead of spending too much time on building or maintaining their brand.

Schools Can Now Provide Additional Benefits for Student Athletes

The NCAA has recently agreed to adopt Transformation Committee recommendations to allow schools to pay more to support a student's academic pursuits, as well as purchase insurance for critical injury, illness, and loss-of-value. Schools are now also able to fund elite-level training, tryouts, and competition for students, which is expected to enhance the overall college athlete experience. With additional funding expected to be channeled into elite-level training, college-level play is expected to become more competitive and intense, which would fuel the trend of more college athletes being drafted into the MLB.

One such benefit is loss-of-value insurance. Loss-of-value insurance refers to a coverage contract that protects an athlete's future contract value from decreasing below a predetermined amount that may be caused by injuries or illnesses suffered during the coverage period. All this forms an attractive package for new players. This means that schools will now be equipped with extra ways to attract new recruits and transfer players alike. As an example of this, when Tyler became a first-round draft selection of the Toronto Blue Jays in 2011, he had an assigned value of $2.75 million. That was Toronto's offer to Tyler. At that time, we as a family were offered an insurance policy by Vanderbilt University but there was an approximately $20,000 premium that we were responsible for. In today's college baseball landscape, a school could offer Tyler both a loss of value insurance policy as well as a policy in case of permanent injury. We may find schools being more conservative in investing in specific students as they are constantly at risk of losing the student to being poached by other schools. For that reason, it will be interesting to see how this new change will play out alongside the one-time penalty-free lateral transfer change.

How Does The MLB Draft Affect College Rosters?

MLB scouts begin scouting for an upcoming draft in late January when JUCO programs begin their season, and then eventually begin to scout college and high school baseball seasons across the country. Living in the Northeast means a later start to the season than the rest of the country. During the early spring of 2011, we as a family did not think that Tyler would be a first-round draft selection. In fact, many draft publications had Tyler somewhere in the second to third round. The 2011 MLB draft is possibly the deepest and strongest draft class in MLB draft history. Every first-round draft selection from the 2011 draft has played at the MLB level. MLB All Stars such as Gerrit Cole, Anthony Rendon, Francisco Lindor, Javier Baez, George Springer, and Sonny Gray were all first round picks.

During Tyler's senior year, he began to gain the attraction of national crosscheckers as well as General Mangers such as Brian Cashman of the Yankees and Theo Epstein, then of the Boston Red Sox. Tyler increasingly began to move up MLB draft boards. Even my former MiLB teammate and scouting director of the Brewers, Bruce Seid, would have drafted Tyler with either the thirteenth or fifteenth overall pick had I not told Bruce in confidence that Tyler was going to honor his commitment to Vanderbilt. Tyler was selected twenty-first overall in the 2011 MLB draft. He was the only first round draft selection that year not to sign. He went on to have a good career at Vanderbilt, winning a College World Series National Championship in 2014, becoming a first-round selection in 2014 by the San Francisco Giants, and earning a degree from Vanderbilt.

A person on the other end of Tyler's experience was Vanderbilt head coach Tim Corbin. A college coach has no control or influence regarding the MLB draft. As you can imagine, Coach Corbin monitored the 2011 draft process closely throughout its entirety. By mid-season of Tyler's senior year of high school, he was calling more frequently to discuss the likelihood of Tyler signing with an MLB team versus honoring his commitment to attend Vanderbilt. This is the high-wire act that college coaches must perform. College coaches not only lose student-athletes already on their rosters to the MLB draft. They also lose recruited student-athletes who choose to sign a professional contract instead of playing college baseball. Many high-profile high school baseball athletes will use the leverage of a high-profile college commitment for a larger signing bonus. Throughout, college coaches must continually fill voids the MLB draft creates on their roster. The draft plays a *major* role in the formation of a college roster.

Number of Rounds Reduced from 40 to 20

In 2020, the MLB draft was shortened from 40 to just 5 rounds to cut costs due to COVID-induced revenue losses. However, instead of returning to the original 40, the 2022 MLB Draft saw only 20 rounds. Future drafts will be expected to remain at 20. Overall, this will mean that teams will be spending much less on players, and the number of spots available for players in the major league draft has thus been reduced by half.

What this means is that the scene will be far more competitive, with athletes having to compete for a smaller number of open spots on teams. Moving forward, greater attention across the nation is expected to be placed on college baseball, as the future of the MLB becomes ever more centered around college student-athletes. As a result, we may also see greater investment into endorsement deals towards student-athletes, leading to a positive feedback loop that will continue to enhance the prestige of college baseball. I feel that it is important for parents that are told that their student-athlete should prepare for the MLB draft. Beginning in 2024/2025 there may be a new MLB draft wrinkle. This wrinkle will even further reduce options for the high school student-athlete. That wrinkle will be the

MLB collective bargaining agreement that calls for an international MLB yearly draft. Under the current agreement, all Latin athletes are free agents and can be signed as young as 16. This current Latin free agent process is filled with greed and MLB cheating the system. Many MLB teams have been fined and executives fired due to mishandling of funds for Latin prospects. MLB wants to level the playing field for all teams by making Latin players part of the MLB draft process. Latin players would now follow Canadian, and Puerto Rican players and now fall under MLB draft guideline and financial draft slots. This will further reduce MLB draft opportunities for US high school athletes and will drive more high school athletes into the world of college baseball.

Draft and Follow Rule Reinstated, Draft Right Retained for a Year

The draft and follow rule allow teams to draft junior college players and retain the rights to draft them for almost a year before actually having to decide whether to sign them. Teams typically do take advantage of this if they are unsure of whether they would want to offer the player a contract. They would then be able to see the player play for another season to get a better understanding of his capabilities, before making the final decision to offer him a contract. It was not unusual for players to improve significantly during this period of time, and teams were also expected to reflect the changes in skill by raising the contract offer. On the other hand, if the team did not choose to sign the player, the player would then be returned into the draft for the following year.

The draft-and-follow rule was eliminated back in 2007 before being reinstated in 2022. This is an effort made by the MLB which would allow for more polished and developed college players to be drafted. With the addition of the draft-and-follow rule, it seems like a minor league system is being created within college baseball, where players may be developed and prepared at the college level for one year. A high school senior or a junior college freshman could now be drafted by an MLB team. Instead of signing that player to a MILB contract, an MLB team can follow that student-athlete for one additional year to see the progress that student-athlete makes before deciding to sign or allow that player to reenter the upcoming MLB draft. They retain draft rights to that player until next year's MLB draft. . The draft-and-follow rule is expected to induce greater competition within all levels of college baseball, which is likely to translate into a better selection of players making it into college baseball. All this points towards enhancing the quality of athletes churned out by the NAIA, NJCAA and NCAA, which further supports the idea that college baseball is gradually becoming the primary source of future major league prospects.

This agglomeration of changes has set in motion a sequence of events that will change college baseball significantly, and there are already instances where we have seen high school athletes being negatively affected. High school athletes must begin to take deeper looks at prospective college programs to ensure that not only will there be room and opportunities at a potential college but also what are the student-athlete retention rates after freshman year as well as how aggressive is a prospective coaching staff in the transfer portal. Both parents and student-athletes need to be better informed, better educated regarding the entire college recruiting process!

NAVIGATING THE SHIFT

To be honest, I am not sure that I could navigate today's youth baseball landscape if I had to do it all over again. In many ways, today's version of youth baseball resembles several pieces of IKEA furniture that you loved in the showroom but must assemble at home by yourself. Unlike IKEA directions, which can make it challenging to understand what goes where and when, allow me to offer you some (hopefully) easy-to-follow directions for your student-athlete. I am going to start, as all directions do, by making sure you have all the necessary parts and tools needed to navigate this process from beginning (youth baseball) to end (college baseball).

Let's face it, this entire process starts in some way, shape, or form at the ages of six through twelve years of age. If I could stand on top of the highest mountain with a real big megaphone to let parents know that there is absolutely no need for travel baseball at these ages, I would. I never played travel baseball, my sons never played travel baseball at those ages, and my grandsons will not be playing travel baseball. Youth baseball starts with a basic understanding of how to catch, throw, and hit a baseball. Much of the early years, six through nine, can be absolutely done locally. These are the ages that children develop the foundation of love and a passion for sport. Allow children to watch baseball. Keep baseball fun and most of all local; most cities and towns across the country offer some form of local youth baseball.

If you are going to look for a local youth program in your area, it will be a great experience for a dad to volunteer to help coach a local team. Don't fall for the "daddy ball is bad" at these young ages. The people telling parents that little league stinks or that it has become "daddy ball" are most likely travel coaches or owners. It is a great life memory for both you as a parent as well as your child to learn the game. It is a great bonding experience as well as a great opportunity to build a foundation of wonderful memories within the sport of baseball.

Youth programs at six through nine should be practice heavy and game light. Maybe a two– to three-practice schedule and one game on Saturdays. Focus on these ages to eliminate fear in your child and replace it with a whole bunch of fun! Create fun drills as a team on how many balls they can catch in a row, how fast they can run to first base, how many ground balls they can field in a row, etc. Practice at these ages can be as short as an hour to ninety minutes. Create competitive fun drills. Any youth program at six through nine that is game intense is a waste of time and resources. Most children at these ages want to be around friends and play multiple sports. Avoid any type of program at these ages that use the words *advanced*, *elite*, and *prospects*! More parents use youth baseball as a social activity at these ages. That may be great for adults, but it's not so much for children. Let them be kids and have fun.

The ages of ten through thirteen, also referred to as the Little League ages, are when the parts and assembly become a bit more challenging. These ages are when travel programs become aggressive. They sell parents on the "quality" of baseball they play and the significance that travel baseball can play regarding a child's opportunities at the high school and college levels. It is true that a number of children at these ages who used to play local Little League are now playing travel youth baseball. The most common sales pitch is that Little League is "daddy ball." I have a news flash for you: so are most of the travel baseball programs at these ages. Here are some red flags to avoid at ten through thirteen: travel programs that are coached by college age athletes, coaches that never played baseball in high school or college, and one coach trying to coach 15-20 players per team. The biggest red flag to avoid at ages ten through thirteen is when a program owner or staff member tells a student-athlete to "get better on your own time—we don't have time for one-on-one instruction. If you need that we offer lessons." If your baseball team at ten through thirteen is not practicing as a team a couple or few times a week and brags about the number of games they play every season, run and avoid!

Now, I can hear many parents reading this and saying, "Walter my son is advanced and needs to be surrounded by similar caliber teammates and competition." Ah, yes, I remember hearing this when Tyler was twelve. I was told countless times, that Tyler "needed" travel baseball and that his little league team was not providing him the challenges and competition he needed to get better. It was nothing more than a used car salesman speech. Parents, if you want to know the simplest way to help your advanced student-athlete become better, let me offer you this piece of advice. Go to your local middle school or high school program and ask them if they need a batboy. Ask if it is possible for your son to watch and occasionally join in on practice. This will cost you nothing, your student-athlete will love and look forward to it, and your local high school coach will get a glimpse of a future student-athlete.

Most travel baseball teams at ten through thirteen end up facing local teams that you could have played locally. Instead you had to drive a few hours away to play a tournament that will have gate fees and concession and souvenir stands, all of which are there to collect your money. To recap ages six through thirteen, keep it local, keep it fun, and keep it practice and repetition heavy. Avoid long distance events, lessons, and any schedule that has more than twenty-five games per season (not including all stars).

That brings me to another important point. I never made an all-star team until I was fifteen; neither did my oldest son, Kyle. Tyler made an all-star team every year from ten on. Kyle and Tyler played in two state championships; they won one. Both boys played at the college level; neither played a day of travel baseball before the age of fourteen. This was not when dinosaurs roamed the earth like when I played. This was 2004–2009. Trust me, my era (1972–1979) was no different than my sons, and their era is no different than your student-athlete's time. The only thing different is the marketing and sales pitch of travel organizations. Practice more and play less organized baseball at these ages. Playing in age groupings such as six to eight, nine to eleven, and twelve to thirteen is by far the best way of helping young players get better! Want to help rebuild youth baseball? Help and volunteer to rebuild the declining Little League and rec programs within local communities. Think of all the money you will save and the fun your athletes will have with their classmates, neighbors, and friends.

Okay, now that we have our foundation built, let's begin to put the important pieces together for those athletes who truly aspire to play baseball beyond the youth levels. It is important to note that many athletes at the ages of thirteen and fourteen give up baseball. This has been the case for many decades. It is nothing new or to be concerned with. Many choose different sports, academic pursuits, musical instruments and, dare I say, time with friends—even those of the romantic variety! As I have stated previously, the number of youth baseball players from six through thirteen is approximately 3.67 million. That number gets reduced to approximately 500,000 from fourteen through eighteen. Many of today's MLB executives are high level academics who played baseball at young ages. They had a passion and a love for the sport, but chose to go down a path based on academic success. Now they call the shots for a major league team.

For the sake of this discussion, we'll assume your son *really* wants to play high school baseball. He also talks about college baseball— okay, now you need insight, you need information, and most of all you need a plan! Here are my thoughts for fourteen through seventeen. First, make sure the travel organization you choose has a track record of developing its own players rather than bringing in "guest" players. It is important that you seek out a team that truly rewards hard-working, talented, and deserving players. Avoid the big money teams where a parent tries to buy playing time for his son and the son's friends. Make sure your travel program has multiple coaches with quality career experience. Coaches that have played or coached at the high school, college or professional level are preferred. If a parent has college or professional experience, that is great and should not be discouraged. Make sure at the ages of fourteen through sixteen that your student-athlete has the option of playing up if his ability level warrants it. A fourteen-year-old will be asked to compete and play with older athletes at the high school level, so now is the time to seek out older competition and practice time with older athletes. Avoid programs that say if they allow your son to play up, they would have to allow other players to play up as well. Playing year by year is a great money-making model, but not a baseball development model.

Good travel programs allow athletes to play multiple positions if they have the ability. They watch and monitor innings for young pitchers. They stress the WE and avoid the ME. They will educate all players on a team during each practice and game. They are not jockeys riding the backs of their athletes. They are helping them understand the extreme difficulty of baseball, their weaknesses more than their strengths, the importance of being where their feet are, moving onto the next pitch rather than stressing about the last pitch, and how important each athlete is to the team. At fourteen through sixteen, make sure your athletes are fully immersed in their strength and nutrition plans and their routines. Any travel program that is not playing a role in developing your student-athlete to become the best that they are capable of being is a waste of both time and money! The name on the jersey is 100% meaningless. Do not pay for the high-profile program that has a history of sending athletes to college.

The only athlete that matters is *yours*. How are they going to develop and prepare your athlete for high school and possibly college baseball? Ask that question! "How are you going to develop and prepare my son?" Those that came before your son are of no concern to your son and his future in the game.

Now for the all-important ages, sixteen through twenty-two. These are the ages that all young athletes and their parents dream of since they put on a pair of spikes and a uniform. Many parents are led to believe that they need to begin to worry about college opportunities, high school playing time, and national travel baseball as soon as their athlete reaches high school. Trust me on this, the most important part of these ages is to come to the full and complete understanding that your athlete's goal should be to trade athletic ability for academic excellence. As a college coach at the NCAA level, I can tell you with complete confidence that college baseball at a lowly level D3 program altered many of my former student-athletes' lives. Many of my former players are now married with children, many of whom are now playing baseball.

A favorite story that I often share with parents that I work with now is that of Keith and Kevin Renaud. These boys were identical twins who were as talented as any player in the country in 2005. Keith was both academically and athletically considered a no doubt NCAA D1 prospect. Kevin, while being equal athletically, was not a college-caliber student academically. When I spoke to their parents, they made it clear that the boys wanted to attend the same college and play together. Keith and Kevin were peanut butter and jelly; they were peas in a pod! They knew each other's next move without uttering a syllable. Mr. Renaud felt that Kevin would never be able to graduate college as he barely graduated high school. Not only did both boys graduate from college, but they also both were NCAA D2 world series participants and regional-national College All Americans. Both are now married with children and have great careers, all due to baseball. The end game of youth baseball is not the MLB. It is not about individual glory or awards. It is for youth baseball to be part of the journey that hopefully doesn't end until after a college career that allows your athlete to collect precious moments and memories. That is what ninety-eight percent of all college baseball athletes are left with, and they are extremely valuable.

For those high school athletes who find themselves to be part of the ten percent of baseball athletes that play at the college level, here is a tip. Many tips I have provided in my book *The Recruiting Process*, but this one you will only find here. With all the changes now at the professional level and NCAA levels, find a college that offers the *real* possibility to compete to get between the lines. The D1-or-bust mentality is simply no longer the correct path. Many student-athletes who play in NAIA and NCAA four-year programs are as talented, if not better, than many D1 athletes. They simply choose to focus on academic strengths, playing time, campus environments, and the collective whole of the college experience. They understand the education and experiences that come with college will last a lifetime. Baseball will not.

The fact is, most baseball players never play beyond high school. Those who do are blessed. They will never forget their teammates, coaches, and that last opportunity to be a part of an organized sport. I will never forget when Tyler came off the mound for the last time as a college student-athlete. As he handed Tim Corbin the baseball after going seven innings in Omaha during the college world series, I saw tears in his eyes. I knew he was aware that his chapter as an amateur athlete was over. A sport he had played since the age of six was about to become his vocation. He would be able to look back on his decision to bypass professional baseball for college baseball and know in his heart that he played a role on a national championship team. He had lived the life of a college student and all that went with that.

It's not about money, accolades, or social media validation. When your little boy puts on the first pair of spikes, uniform, and hat, it is about enjoying the ride and all that comes with it. No amount of money can buy a college roster spot or professional opportunity. Baseball is about moments; some little boys succeed in their moment's and others may fail. That is baseball and that is life. The sooner your son learns how hard both life and baseball truly are, the better prepared he will be for each day of his life

IF I COULD WAVE A MAGIC BASEBALL BAT

Over the last few years, I have often been asked what changes I would make if I were able to wave a magic bat over the current state of baseball. Many folks tell me "Well the genie is out of the bottle" or, my favorite, "the toothpaste is out of the tube." That may be the case with the current state of baseball as well. Travel baseball is here to stay, college baseball has become the ultimate destination for parents, and student-athletes and professional baseball seems heck bent on succumbing to the "instant gratification–speed of the game" mantra. So, if you would allow me to share them, here are my hopes, wishes, and dreams for the great sport of baseball.

If I were allowed to sit and chat with Theo Epstein or Rob Manfred, I would make the following suggestions. First, I would ask that all MLB personnel make themselves available to the younger fans. Make appearances at local elementary schools and little leagues. Help bring back a connection to the little boys and girls who are the game's future. Share their personal journeys from Little League to the Big Leagues. I would also choose a few dates each year for children to play catch and interact with their favorite professional players or parents on a minor or major league field. Allow the children to feel and see what these fields look like from a player's viewpoint. There has become a massive disconnect between professional players and children. Allowing children access, even in a brief capacity, encourages children to dream and to find childhood heroes.

I would ask MLB to offer a "coach the coaches" video program that could be shared via Little League and local rec leagues at the game's youngest levels (six to twelve years old). Let's have MLB work with Little League to create a smaller and softer baseball. A smaller ball allows little hands to fit the baseball. Football does this with its pee wee, junior, and youth sizes; baseball can do the same. The softer ball would also help teach children proper fielding skills and ease fear. Both things would allow and encourage children to play catch more often. My last request for MLB would be to help create real baseball academies that would simply teach children the game in both a classroom and on-field capacity. Academies would give children access to learning the game in a consistent manner. That would increase participation and help their understanding of the essence of the game. It would allow children to become better-informed fans.

The sport of baseball at the college level may never catch the amount of interest that football and basketball have, but it has truly begun to play a much larger role financially within college athletics. Each year and across different levels of college baseball, attendance and television contracts continue to grow. There are many forthcoming positive changes within the college baseball landscape that I already discussed in previous chapters. But there is one major change that I would like to see throughout college baseball: greater access for parents and student-athletes to see firsthand what being a college baseball player is like. I guess my best analogy would be a "take your child to work" day. College athletics must be better understood by both student-athletes and their families. Let's let aspiring athletes live what really occurs each day as a college student-athlete.

I firmly believe if a younger student-athlete could see what it looks, sounds, and feels like to be a college student-athlete, it would reduce the number who transfer or drop out. The illusion and hype of college baseball seen by today's middle and high school student-athletes is sending the wrong message. To play baseball at the college level is truly a challenge. The real opportunity that college athletics presents to high school athletes is education. There's a reason employers look at a former college student-athlete with a higher regard. A college student-athlete shows accountability, discipline, and most importantly dedication to a team. We often think college baseball will lead to stardom and opportunities at the professional levels. This is simply not the case for over ninety-seven percent of college athletes. Think of all the student-athletes in all sports who play on television in large conferences such as the SEC, ACC, PAC-12, Big-12, and Big-10. These athletes play at the highest amateur level, but only a fraction of these athletes ever make a living playing a sport. What they are really doing is trading athletic excellence for academic opportunity. The biggest issue in the college baseball landscape is the fact that many athletes will not graduate or if they do are saddled with large amounts of student debt. Many parents and student-athletes that chase the big programs do not understand that many private colleges and universities are well over sixty thousand dollars a year. If a student-athlete is talented and receives a 50% scholarship, they will be left to pay over one hundred twenty thousand dollars upon graduation. That is equivalent to a mortgage payment. Look for a program that is affordable, that offers the best possible financial aid package and best academic degree.

I saved the biggest challenge for last. This is a magic wand I wish I could wave. Many people hear me opine week after week about the current state of youth baseball. I want to finish this book with a few personal wishes that I hope find their way back to the younger levels of baseball. When I speak with parents and younger athletes, I often ask who their favorite players or teams are. I do this as a way of gaining an understanding of an athlete's passion and a parents understanding of the sport. If this is my magic wand, then I want to make sure that you, as a reader, understand where my passion, my love for the game comes from.

People often laugh when I tell them how bad I was as a kid. There is no need for embellishment or exaggeration. I simply grew up in a family of non-athletes. Not an athletic bone in any family member's body or DNA. I grew up in a city that has a rich history of producing prominent professional athletes in all sports. In fact, if you did a google search of professional athletes from Lynn, Massachusetts, you will find an extremely long list. For me as a kid, there was only one who altered my life. His name was Tony Conigliaro. My path crossed his one day at Lynn playground after he had retired. He had just given a talk to a local Little League program and was standing behind the backstop talking to a coach. I simply was about to get on my bike to head home after a pickup game. As I hoped on my brown Schwinn bike with my bat across the handlebars, I hear a voice "hey kid, who's bat do you have?"

Now, I was not on a little league team at the time. I was nine and only played baseball at the sandlot level with school and neighborhood friends. To say that, in 1972, Tony C was larger than life would be a gross understatement. Tony C was John Wayne, Batman, The Lone Ranger, and Mr. Brady, all wrapped into one. So as one might imagine, as I turned around to answer the question about my bat and saw my childhood idol standing at *my* playground, my eyes opened as wide as the moon on an October fall evening and suddenly my throat was Mojave Desert dry! As I began to stutter and try to utter just a syllable, this icon started walking towards me. He extended his hand and asked to see my bat.

A quick back story is needed. In 1972 aluminum bats were not available, at least not in my neck of the woods. Back then we had Louisville Slugger wood bats that might have been sold in places like Rich's or Sear's department stores. My bat was given to me by my neighbor, Mr. Scarborough. He was going to throw it away because it had a crack in it but gave it to me instead. I took the bat home, put a few nails in it, and wrapped the cracked area with black electrical tape. As I handed Mr. Conigliaro the bat, he smiled and said, "Great choice kid! Can you hit? You know, to be a good hitter you have to squeeze something like this everywhere you go!" He then pulled out greenish tennis ball out of his sweatshirt and flipped it to me—me! "Here kid, take this and remember if you want to be a good hitter, you need strong wrists and forearms. Keep squeezing it wherever you go!" As he walked away and I jumped on my bike, at that very moment I knew two things. I was going to be a baseball player, and no matter where I went, I was going to have that tennis ball in my hand.

You might be wondering, what does this have to do with the magic wand Walter? The baseball bug had bitten me. From that exact moment, nothing mattered more to me than playing, watching, and talking baseball. If I was going to get better, I needed to practice. I found ways to do things on my own, whether it was bouncing balls off my grandmother's chimney or front steps for hours at a time or hitting acorns and rocks with my bat into the woods, I was doing something related to baseball. As I got older, the older kids in the neighborhood allowed me to play with them. It was mostly right field, but I was *on the field*! I was surrounded by older, bigger, and *much* better players. I watched and copied *every* move they made. These kids would often emulate MLB players by pitching like Luis "El Tiante" Tiant, hitting like Fred Lynn, or copying the hitting stances of Carl Yastrzemski and Dwight Evans. I never had a formal lesson in my life and did not play organized youth baseball until I was ten years old. At ten, I was not good enough for the Majors division of little league and had to play B Farm or minors division. Much of what I learned as a young athlete was by watching older and better players. It helped show me the way to become a better player. It allowed me to learn to smaller components of the game and how to implement them into my body and mind.

Therefore, my first wave of the wand at the youth level would be to bring back multiple ages playing with and against each other. For multiple decades before and after I played, Little League, Babe Ruth, and American Legion produced great athletes across all levels of baseball. Bring back age groupings such as 7U–8U, 9U–11U, 13U–

14U, and 15U–18U. This would allow children to return to learning from their peer groups and allow a better caliber of play. As I stated earlier in this chapter, there needs to be a smaller baseball designed for the younger age groups. I would even suggest the creation of a newer division of youth baseball called "The Little Sluggers League." Little Sluggers would be for 4U–6U players, with the newly created smaller and softer baseball, lighter and bigger barreled Wiffle ball–style bats, and no gloves needed. It would simply be children throwing, hitting, and running for 45– to 60-minute games. We need to introduce the sport to children in a fun environment that does not have screaming, yelling, or competition. Travel baseball as young as six years of age is simply silly. The sport of baseball needs to be *inclusive* at younger ages and not *exclusive*.

My second wave of the wand at the youth level would be to return the game to kids as participants and athletes, instead of as customers being served by travel owners and their facilities. Youth sports from the ages of four through thirteen should be open to all. No child should be denied an opportunity to participate in youth sports, in this case baseball, because of lack of money or access to equipment. We should take advantage of the recycling-driven world we currently live in. Pass equipment on to younger athletes so they can participate in their local leagues. Once they have equipment, they'll need a league that focuses on practices and teaching the game. I know giving back is something that is important to many former players and coaches. We can help youth baseball move away from the "put a dollar in my pocket and I will teach you" environment. Let's make it easier for the parent volunteers in local leagues by helping them understand how to run a practice. Show them what drills can be done to help the children learn at the younger levels.

My third and final wave of the baseball wand would be to create a program that would go into elementary schools across the country and encourage Little League or local rec ball sign-ups. The numbers across local Little Leagues are dwindling and that is a fact. Many people want to simply chalk that up to the emergence of travel baseball, but it is a much larger problem. Local fields that once were filled with pickup or sandlot games are now used by other sports or local travel teams. Many of these fields are locked and do not allow local children access. In some extreme cases, old fields have been sold to home builders. We need to go where the children are at the ages of five through twelve, and that is the elementary schools. Create fun events. Have a play catch with mom or dad day; hold hit, field, and throw competitions; and build back youth baseball at a community level. Make local leagues meaningful. Allow children to discover and learn about the game of baseball through their communities. Allow them to develop a passion for the game, to follow their local team, and even to have childhood heroes. If we as adults simply create a plan and act at younger ages, maybe children will find their way back to the sport.

Now I know many people think the toothpaste is out of the tube; travel baseball has become too big now, and there is no way of returning to the days of Little League. What if we made travel baseball at the ages of six through eleven become part of Little League? What if we combined local cities and towns into one Little League charter? Have one weeknight game a week and a double header on Saturday. Instead of driving hours for travel baseball, travel to a neighboring city or town like in a high school playing season. If we spend enough time discussing and thinking of ideas to return the game of baseball to the children at younger ages, I am positive we will see numbers increase at the local and Little League levels.

Right now, we are taking the things that make sense for adults or older student-athletes and applying them to children. Children live and learn by the guidance and structure provided by adults, but children do not understand the world of travel baseball. Children always want to have their parents' approval as well as to make their parents happy, but they do not understand baseball lessons at six through ten. They do, however, understand playing with friends. It is a part of childhood. Playing with friends teaches life lessons such as sharing, being a part of a group, and conflict resolution. Children have been learning these lessons for centuries without adult interaction. Yet the world has suddenly decided on behalf of children that life needs to be scripted, children need routine, and most of all children need to hurry up and decide who and what they want to be by the age of twelve. You might laugh at that, but have you ever looked on social media and see parents promoting their child's decision to attend a university at fourteen? Adults now want to focus on their child's destination within youth sports instead of simply allowing them to enjoy their journey. It is *their* journey. Let's return the sport of baseball to the children. Allow them to develop friendships filled with moments and memories. Baseball and life have so much in common. Through baseball, children learn both physically and mentally how to fall, fail, get back up, and try again. Let's return the game back to them. Who knows, maybe they will once again ride bikes to a local field to play a pickup game. Maybe they'll run across a former Major League player who offers them a tip, and when they grow up, maybe they will write a book just like this.

ABOUT THE AUTHOR

Walter Beede

With a baseball career that has spanned over forty years, Walter Beede brings a diverse background to parents and student-athletes. His highlights as an athlete include All New  England First Team high school player. He received a scholarship from Arizona State University and was selected in the Round 13 of the 1981 MLB draft by the Chicago Cubs. He has been a head coach at the high school, American Legion, National Travel Baseball and NCAA levels. He has also worked as a Task Force member for the prestigious Team USA program in Cary, NC.

The parent of two sons who competed and graduated at the college level, Walter has been through the recruiting process with both of his sons, Kyle, and Tyler. Kyle played for LSU Eunice and LSU Alexandria, and Tyler played for the National Champion Vanderbilt Commodores. Tyler holds the distinction of being the only New England player in the fifty-seven-year history of the MLB draft to be a two-time, first-round selection.

Drawing from his experiences as a player, evaluator, head coach, and parent, Walter helps student-athletes and families navigate the challenges of amateur baseball—from the playing season and the recruiting process to athlete evaluations. Walter has helped more than 700 athletes from across the country over the last twenty-five years and has developed an extensive coaching and MLB scout network.

CPSIA information can be obtained
at www.ICGtesting.com
Printed in the USA
LVHW071655070123
736535LV00012B/182